Comptroller of the Currency
Administrator of National Banks

Insurance Activities

Comptroller's Handbook

June 2002

Management

Insurance Activities

Table of Contents

Overview

This "Insurance Activities" handbook booklet provides information for bankers and national bank examiners on the risks, controls and supervision of national banks' insurance activities by the OCC. This booklet provides examiners guidance on performing appropriate assessments of risks to national banks from insurance activities, including a process that may be used in planning and conducting risk assessments.[1] Because of the complexity and importance of the legal requirements associated with insurance activities, this handbook also contains considerable legal guidance.

National banks have conducted insurance sales activities since the early 1900s. The types of insurance products and services offered and the associated distribution systems are changing significantly as this business line evolves. In recent years, national banks have engaged in insurance activities as a means to increase profitability mainly through expanding and diversifying fee-based income. Banks are also interested in providing broader financial services to customers by expanding their insurance product offerings.

The Gramm-Leach-Bliley Act of 1999 (GLBA) is important legislation that addresses a number of significant issues affecting both national banks and the examination process. Among its provisions, GLBA reaffirms the authority of national banks and their subsidiaries to sell insurance. The law also clarifies the regulatory structure and product offerings related to national bank insurance activities.

GLBA establishes a functional regulatory framework that reaffirms the states' authority to regulate insurance activities conducted within banks and through a functionally regulated affiliate (FRA).[2] FRAs can be either bank affiliates or bank subsidiaries. Additionally, GLBA reaffirms the OCC's responsibility for evaluating the consolidated risk profile of the national bank. This evaluation

---

[1] The OCC does not consider debt cancellation contracts, debt suspension agreements, and fixed and variable rate annuities as insurance products within the scope of the guidance and policies in this handbook.

[2] An FRA is an affiliate (including subsidiary) of a bank that is regulated by the SEC, CFTC, or a state insurance regulator, but generally does not include a bank holding company, savings and loan holding company, or a depository institution.

includes determining the risks posed to the bank from insurance activities and the effectiveness of the bank's risk management systems, including compliance with banking laws and applicable consumer protection requirements. This handbook booklet contains the OCC's process for assessing risks to the national bank from insurance activities. This risk assessment process is consistent with GLBA's functional regulation requirements and will be conducted at the bank level. It is anticipated that the OCC's examinations of FRAs will be infrequent.

National Bank Insurance Powers

Both federal and state laws may govern national bank insurance activities.

Authority Under Federal Law

A national bank is authorized to engage in insurance agency activities under 12 USC 92. Under 12 USC 92, a national bank that is "located and doing business in any place[3] the population of which does not exceed five thousand . . . may . . . act as the agent for any fire, life, or other insurance company." Under this authority, a national bank may sell most types of insurance from an agency located in a "place of 5,000" or fewer inhabitants. There are no geographic restrictions on the bank's ability to solicit and serve its insurance customers. National banks are not, however, authorized to sell title insurance under 12 USC 92. National banks' authority to sell title insurance is based on GLBA section 303 (15 USC 6713). See "Permissible National Bank Insurance Activities" section of the handbook for a discussion of a national bank's authority to sell title insurance under GLBA.

National banks also may engage in various insurance agency activities under 12 USC 24(Seventh). This law authorizes national banks to engage in the "business of banking," and to exercise "all such incidental powers as shall be necessary to carry on the business of banking." Although an insurance product sold under this authority could also be sold under 12 USC 92, there are no geographic "place of 5,000" limits under 12 USC 24(Seventh). National banks also may engage in insurance agency activities without geographic restriction through their financial subsidiaries[4] established under GLBA section 121 (12 USC 24a).

---

[3] An area designated as a "place" by the Census Bureau is acknowledged as a "place" by the OCC for 12 USC 92 purposes. The Census Bureau defines "place" to include both incorporated places and census designated places.
[4] A financial subsidiary is any company that is controlled by one or more insured depository

National banks are authorized under GLBA section 302 (15 USC 6712) to provide insurance as principal (underwriter or reinsurer) for any product the OCC had approved for national banks prior to January 1, 1999, or that national banks were lawfully providing as of January 1, 1999. Refer to the "Permissible National Bank Insurance Activities" section of this booklet for a discussion of a national bank's authority to provide insurance as principal under GLBA.

Applicability of State Laws

In 1945, Congress passed the McCarran-Ferguson Act, granting states the power to regulate most aspects of the insurance business. The McCarran-Ferguson Act (15 USC 1012(b)) states that "no act of Congress shall be construed to invalidate, impair, or supersede any law enacted by any state for the purpose of regulating the business of insurance, or which imposes a fee or tax upon such business, unless such Act specifically relates to the business of insurance." Therefore, under the McCarran-Ferguson Act, a state statute enacted for the purpose of regulating the business of insurance preempts a conflicting federal statute, unless the federal statute specifically relates to the business of insurance. As a result of this law, national banks must be cognizant of the potential applicability of state law requirements.

The extent to which states could regulate national bank insurance activities authorized by federal law was clarified in 1996 by preemption principles that were applied by the U.S. Supreme Court in Barnett Bank of Marion County, NA v. Nelson, 517 U.S. 25 (1996). Under Barnett and the substantial body of law upon which the Barnett Court relied, state laws that prevent, impair, impede, or hamper the exercise of national bank powers, or that discriminate against national banks, are preempted. As a result of GLBA, the standards for determining when state laws are preempted became more complex. Under GLBA, state laws generally cannot "prevent or restrict" insurance activities conducted by national banks and their subsidiaries. For insurance sales, solicitations, and cross marketing, however, state laws cannot "prevent or significantly interfere" with bank and subsidiary insurance activities, in accordance with the legal standards for preemption set forth in Barnett.

---

institutions, other than a subsidiary that: (i) engages solely in activities that national banks may engage in directly and that are conducted subject to the same terms and conditions that govern the conduct of these activities by national banks; or (ii) a national bank is specifically authorized to control by the express terms of a federal statute, and not by implication or interpretation. Financial subsidiaries may engage in activities that are not permissible for the parent bank, as long as the activities are financial in nature. See 12 CFR 5.39.

GLBA also provides 13 areas or "safe harbors,"[5] within which the states can regulate insurance sales, solicitation, and cross marketing practices of banks and their subsidiaries and affiliates. Those 13 safe harbors cover advertising practices, licensing requirements, various notices and disclaimers, tying, restrictions on paying fees to non-licensed employees, and other potentially coercive sales practices.

A state law concerning insurance sales, solicitation, and cross-marketing activities that does not fit within the safe harbors is treated in one of two ways, depending on when the law was enacted. The traditional Barnett preemption principles apply to all state laws for insurance sales, solicitation, and cross-marketing activities that do not fit within one or more of the safe harbors. State laws regulating those activities enacted on or after September 3, 1998 are subject to the Barnett preemption principles and a new anti-discrimination standard.

Application of those principles can create novel and complex legal issues that the OCC reviews case by case. In October 2001, the OCC published its first opinion letter, analyzing whether a state's insurance sales laws would be preempted pursuant to the Barnett standards as incorporated in section 104 of GLBA. See 66 Federal Register 51502 (Oct. 9, 2001). That letter contains a comprehensive discussion of how the standards apply. Until the law in this area becomes settled, however, questions about whether particular provisions of state insurance sales laws apply to national banks should be referred to the OCC's Law Department.

Permissible National Bank Insurance Activities

Examiners should consult with the OCC's Law Department if any questions arise concerning the permissibility of national banks to engage in specific insurance activities. Examples of insurance activities permissible for national banks and their subsidiaries include:

Insurance Activities as Agent

- Selling insurance as agent from a "place of 5,000" consistent with 12 USC 92. A national bank may act as a general insurance agent and sell most types of insurance from any office located in a community of 5,000 or less. No geographic restrictions limit the bank's ability to solicit and serve

---

[5] Refer to GLBA 104(d)(2)(B), 15 USC 6701(d)(2)(B), for the 13 safe harbors.

its insurance customers. A national bank is not generally authorized to sell title insurance under 12 USC 92, but may sell title insurance to the extent permitted under GLBA, as discussed later. In some states, insurance agency activities authorized under 12 USC 92 may be characterized as managing general agency (MGA) activities.

- Selling title insurance, as authorized under GLBA. Under GLBA, a national bank or its operating subsidiary may sell title insurance in a state where a state bank is permitted to sell title insurance, but only in the same manner and to the same extent as the state bank. Also, a national bank and its subsidiary may conduct title insurance activities that the national bank or the subsidiary was actively and lawfully conducting before November 12, 1999. Neither a national bank nor its operating subsidiaries may offer, sell, or underwrite title insurance, if a state law was in effect before November 12, 1999 that prohibits those activities in that state. Although financial subsidiaries are not subject to those title insurance sales restrictions, they may not underwrite title insurance.

- Selling crop insurance, as authorized under 12 USC 92 and 12 USC 24a. A bank's sales of crop insurance are permitted from a "place of 5,000" consistent with 12 USC 92. Under 12 USC 24a, a national bank is authorized to sell crop insurance as agent through the bank's financial subsidiary.

- Selling insurance as agent without geographic limitation through a financial subsidiary, as authorized under 12 USC 24a. Financial subsidiaries of a national bank are authorized under 12 USC 24a to act as an insurance agent for all types of insurance, in any state.

- Selling credit-related insurance as agent under 12 USC 24(Seventh). Pursuant to 12 USC 24(Seventh), national banks or their subsidiaries may sell credit-related insurance products, including:

  — credit life insurance (as defined in 12 CFR 2.2(b));
  — involuntary unemployment insurance (protects the bank if the borrower becomes involuntarily unemployed);
  — vendors single interest insurance and double interest insurance (insures the bank or the bank and the borrower, respectively, against loss or damage to personal property pledged as loan collateral);
  — mechanical breakdown insurance (protects a loan customer against most major mechanical failures during the loan's life); and,

— vehicle service contracts (protects the value of loan collateral from mechanical breakdown for the term of the contract).

Insurance Activities as Principal

- Providing insurance as principal (underwriter or reinsurer). GLBA permits national banks and their subsidiaries to provide insurance as principal (underwriter or reinsurer) for any product that the OCC had approved for national banks prior to January 1, 1999, or that national banks were lawfully providing as of January 1, 1999. Included among the various types of insurance that national banks and their subsidiaries may provide as principal are credit-related insurance, municipal bond insurance, safe deposit box insurance, self insurance of business risk insurance, and private mortgage insurance. Examiners should consult with the OCC's Law Department if they have questions on whether national banks may provide other types of insurance as principal.

Insurance Activities as Finder

- Acting as finder. Insurance finder activities are authorized for national banks under 12 USC 24(Seventh) as part of the business of banking.[6] The OCC has also permitted banks acting as finders to provide extensive billing services to process insurance forms.

Bank Structures for National Bank Insurance Activities

A national bank may structure its insurance activities using one or a combination of legal entities. These include conducting insurance activities through the bank directly, a related insurance entity, or an unaffiliated third party. Each structure has certain benefits and efficiencies; a bank's choice will likely depend upon its resources and strategic preferences. Each of these structures must comply with appropriate legal requirements.[7]

---

[6] Some state laws may treat finder activities as activities that constitute acting as an insurance agent under state law. Where a state law characterized finder activities as activities of an insurance agent, national banks should comply with the applicable state insurance licensing and other requirements.
[7] Certain variable life insurance products are securities registered with the Securities Exchange Commission (SEC). These products are sold through broker/dealers whose functional regulator is the SEC. The SEC may use self-regulatory organizations, such as the National Association of Securities Dealers Regulation (NASDR) and the New York Stock Exchange (NYSE), to fulfill its regulatory responsibility.

Bank Direct Sales

In many states, a national bank must obtain a license — that is, the bank is the "licensed agency," and individuals working in the bank are licensed agents. Other states may require only that the individual be licensed. A bank that conducts its own insurance sales or operations may be able to exercise more control over the insurance activities than it would if it used a separate corporate or third-party structure. No formal application with the OCC is required, if insurance activities are conducted directly through the bank.

Investment in an Insurance Entity

A national bank may choose to invest in an insurance entity, either through a controlling interest in an operating subsidiary or a financial subsidiary or a non-controlling interest in another enterprise. A bank's investment in an insurance entity may involve acquiring an existing entity or starting up a de novo entity. National banks planning to invest in an insurance entity should consult 12 CFR 5 for the appropriate corporate filing procedures with the OCC. A national bank may also use a holding company affiliate to offer insurance products and services to its clients.

Several factors may influence a bank's decision to invest in an insurance entity. Establishment of a separate corporation for insurance activities may minimize the potential legal liability to the bank from financial losses arising from the subsidiary's insurance activities. In addition, in the event that the bank purchases an existing insurance entity, the necessary expertise and an existing customer base can be acquired immediately.

Operating Subsidiary

National banks are authorized to conduct insurance activities in an operating subsidiary. A national bank's operating subsidiary may be structured as a corporation, a limited liability company, or a similar entity. The parent national bank must own more than 50 percent of the voting (or similar type of controlling) interest in the operating subsidiary, or may hold 50 percent or less if the parent bank otherwise controls the subsidiary and no other party controls more than a majority interest in the subsidiary. See 12 CFR 5.34 for additional information.

Financial Subsidiary

GLBA permits national banks to own financial subsidiaries that may engage in many activities financial in nature or incidental thereto, including insurance agency activities. Financial subsidiaries are authorized to act as an insurance agent for all types of insurance, including title insurance, from any location, and are not confined to a "place of 5,000." See 12 CFR 5.39 for additional information.

Non-controlling Investment

Twelve CFR 5.36 provides that national banks may own, either directly or indirectly, a non-controlling interest in an enterprise. The enterprise may be a corporation, limited partnership, limited liability company, or similar entity. A non-controlling investment represents another structural option that banks may consider as a vehicle to offer insurance products and services. National banks that make non-controlling investments must meet the following four-part test:

- Activities of the enterprise must be part of, or incidental to, the business of banking, or otherwise authorized for a national bank.

- The bank must be able to prevent the entity from engaging in activities that do not meet this standard or otherwise be able to withdraw its investment.

- The bank's loss exposure must be limited with no open-ended liability.

- The investment must be convenient or useful to the bank in carrying out its business and may not be a mere passive investment unrelated to the national bank's business.

Holding Company Affiliate

Some banking organizations structure their insurance activities directly under the holding company. GLBA permits a broader range of insurance activities under this structure including broader insurance underwriting authority. A national bank may contract with the holding company affiliate to offer insurance products and services to its client base. Such transactions between a bank and a holding company affiliate must comply with the standards of Section 23B of the Federal Reserve Act. In other words, such transactions must be on terms and under circumstances that are substantially the same, or at least as favorable to the bank, as those prevailing at the time for comparable transactions with or involving other nonaffiliated companies; or in the absence of comparable transactions, on terms and under circumstances that in good faith would be offered to or would apply to, nonaffiliated companies. Generally, this requirement means that the transactions must be conducted on an arm's-length basis, and the bank must receive at least fair market value for any services it provides to its affiliate.

Arrangements with Unaffiliated Third Parties

Banks may elect to enter into agreements with third parties that have no affiliation with the bank. These arrangements can provide banks with expertise and services that otherwise would have to be developed in-house or purchased. Depending upon the type of insurance being sold, the expected volume of business, and the size of the bank, banks may find that using unaffiliated third parties to be more advantageous than establishing bank-direct or bank affiliated insurance programs. Additionally, some banks may elect to offer more specialized products through an arrangement that may or may not involve common ownership or affiliation.

Distribution Methods

Within the authorized structures, banks may use various methods to distribute their insurance products. The sales force could involve fully dedicated agents or part-time agents. Part-time agents generally are part of a bank's platform program and may be authorized to sell bank and insurance products. These agents may have multiple employers, which may include the bank, an insurance agency, and a securities broker. Distribution methods may include face-to-face customer meetings, seminars, telemarketing, direct mail, referrals, the Internet, and other electronic media.

Agency Activities and the Role of the Insurance Agent

No one in the insurance business deals more closely with the public than insurance agents. Consumer confidence in the insurance industry depends on the demonstrated knowledge, experience, and professionalism of the insurance agent with whom a customer chooses to do business. An agent is someone who has been authorized by an insurance company to represent it. The insurance company (or insurer) underwrites and issues policies. The agent's role includes:

- Describing the insurance company's policies to prospective customers.
- Soliciting applications for insurance.
- Providing service to prospects and policyholders.
- Collecting premiums (when authorized) from policyholders and applicants.

Agents are most commonly described in terms of the contractual relationship between the agent and an insurance company. An exclusive agent is an individual who represents only one insurance company and is often, but not always, an employee of that insurer. A general agent is usually contractually awarded a specific geographic territory for an individual insurance company. General agents build their own agency and usually represent only one insurer. Unlike exclusive agents, who usually receive a salary in addition to commissions, general agents are paid by commissions only. An independent agent can work alone or in partnership or corporate affiliations. Under a contractual agreement, independent agents represent many different insurers in the life, health, and property and liability fields. All of their compensation is from commissions.

Managing General Agency (MGA) and the Role of an MGA

An MGA is a wholesaler of insurance products and services to insurance agents. An MGA receives contractual authority from an insurer to assume many of the insurance company's functions. The MGA may provide insurance products through local insurance agents. The MGA may also provide diversified services, including marketing, accounting, data processing, policy maintenance and service, and monitoring of claims. Many insurance companies prefer the MGA distribution and management system for the marketing and underwriting of their insurance products, because it avoids the high cost of establishing a branch office. Most states require that an MGA be licensed.

Finders Activities and the Role of the Finder

A national bank may act as a finder to bring together potential purchasers and sellers of insurance. As a finder, a national bank may receive a fee to identify potential parties, inquire about interest, introduce or arrange meetings of interested parties, and otherwise bring parties together for a transaction that the parties themselves negotiate and consummate.

Reinsurance and the Role of the Reinsurer

Reinsurance is insurance for insurers. As individuals and businesses purchase insurance as protection from the consequences of loss, so do insurers. Reinsurance allows an original insurer, also called the direct writer or ceding company, to reduce its underwriting risk by transferring all or part of the risk under an insurance policy or a group of policies to another company or insurer, known as the reinsurer. The original insurer may retain only a portion of the risk and reinsure the balance with a second company. The reinsurer then assumes that portion of the risk and receives a portion of the premium.

In establishing a reinsurance arrangement, the insurer should seek a reinsurer that shares its underwriting discipline and that operates under comparable standards. The same is true for reinsurers seeking partners among insurers. Banks that have captive reinsurance subsidiaries that reinsure all or part of private mortgage insurance for real estate loans also must conduct their activities in compliance with the requirements of the Real Estate Settlement Procedures Act (RESPA), 24 CFR 3500.

Regulation and Supervision

The OCC is responsible for supervising the safety and soundness of the national banking system. This responsibility encompasses evaluating the consolidated risk profile of the national bank, including determining the potential material risks posed to the bank by the functionally regulated activities of a national bank's subsidiaries and affiliates. The OCC will assess the risks posed to the bank from its insurance related activities by using a risk assessment process that is consistent with GLBA's functional regulation requirements. The assessment is integrated into the OCC's normal supervisory process and embraces the supervision by risk approach in determining the necessity, frequency, and depth of the analysis. The assessment will be conducted at the bank level, and it is anticipated that the OCC's examinations of FRAs will be infrequent.

This section contains information on the OCC's supervisory process involving functionally regulated activities. It identifies the risks and significant legal requirements applicable to national banks' insurance activities. The OCC's assessment process is detailed in the "Risk Assessment Process" section of this booklet.

Functionally Regulated Activities

GLBA codified the concept of "functional regulation," recognizing the role of the state insurance commissioners, the Securities and Exchange Commission (SEC), and the Commodities Futures Trading Commission as the primary regulators of insurance, securities, and commodities activities, respectively.

The state insurance regulators are responsible for enforcing individual state's laws on the insurance companies and their associated agencies and agents doing business in the state. States regulate, among other things, licensing insurance agents or agencies, the financial stability of insurance companies, marketing and trade practices, the content of insurance policies, and the setting of premium rates. Each state has its own legal requirements and supervisory methods. State insurance regulators refer to the National Association of Insurance Commissioners (NAIC) model laws for guidance in drafting state regulations.[8]

As the primary regulator of national banks, the OCC has the responsibility for evaluating the consolidated risk profile of a bank. This responsibility includes determining the potential material risks posed to the bank by functionally regulated activities conducted by the bank or by an FRA, such as an affiliate insurance agency. A key component of this assessment is evaluating a national bank's systems for monitoring and controlling risks posed by functionally regulated activities conducted in the bank or an FRA. The OCC is also responsible for determining compliance with applicable legal requirements under the OCC's jurisdiction.

The assessment of risk at individual national banks must adhere to GLBA requirements that limit the OCC's authority to obtain reports directly from and examine an FRA, unless certain conditions exist. GLBA does not limit the OCC's authority to obtain reports from or examine the national bank itself. If the risk assessment identifies potential significant risk to the bank from the FRA's insurance activities, the OCC will seek additional information or reports from the appropriate functional regulator. If such information or report is not made available, the OCC may seek to obtain it from the FRA if the information or report is necessary to assess:

---

[8] The NAIC consists of principal insurance regulatory authorities from each state and its primary function is to develop uniform standards for the insurance industry. State insurance regulators have discretion in implementing the NAIC's recommendations given the NAIC has no authority over its individual members.

- A material risk to the affiliated national bank;

- Compliance with a federal law the OCC has specific jurisdiction to enforce with respect to the insurance entity; or

- The system for monitoring and controlling operational and financial risks that may pose a threat to the safety and soundness of the affiliated national bank.

GLBA does not, however, limit the OCC's authority to seek information on an FRA in the possession of the bank or from sources other than the FRA to the extent needed to evaluate the risks an FRA poses to the bank.

GLBA also imposes limitations on the OCC's ability to directly examine insurance activities conducted by FRAs. The OCC may directly examine the FRA only when:

- There is reasonable cause to believe that the company is engaged in activities that pose a material risk to the affiliated national bank;

- After reviewing relevant reports, a reasonable determination is made that an examination of the company is necessary to adequately inform the OCC of the system for monitoring and controlling operational and financial risks that may pose a threat to the safety and soundness of the affiliated national bank; or

- Based on reports and other information available, there is reasonable cause to believe that the company is not in compliance with federal law that the OCC has specific jurisdiction to enforce against the company, including provisions relating to transactions with affiliates, and the OCC cannot make such determination through examination of the national bank.

Before an examiner requests information from or conducts an examination of an FRA or an unaffiliated third-party insurance provider,[9] the examiner should discuss the circumstances with the appropriate deputy comptroller. Also, the examiner should consult the appropriate deputy comptroller prior

---

[9] Although GLBA limits on bank regulators' ability to examine and obtain reports technically apply only to affiliated entities, the OCC will generally apply the same principles when seeking information from an unaffiliated third-party insurance provider.

to contacting the functional regulator for additional information on the FRA's or unaffiliated third party's insurance activities.

GLBA functional regulation limitations on obtaining reports and examinations do not apply to insurance activities conducted directly by the bank. In those arrangements, the state insurance regulator is responsible for functional regulation of the bank's insurance activities. The OCC is responsible for supervising the safety and soundness of those insurance activities and for evaluating compliance with banking law requirements.

Effective functional supervision places a premium on close cooperation and coordination among the various regulators. The OCC has entered into information sharing agreements[10] with many state insurance departments to assist in this coordination and is working toward entering into agreements with all states. Large bank EICs and ADCs with portfolio responsibilities should maintain open channels of communication with their state insurance regulatory counterparts and work directly with them on institution-specific issues. These efforts can result in strengthening regulatory oversight and reducing the burden of overlapping jurisdiction on the regulated entities. This includes the coordination of supervisory activities, communication of critical issues, and exchange of necessary information. When an OCC examiner receives a request for information from another functional regulator, the examiner should consult the appropriate deputy comptroller and provide the deputy comptroller with a copy of the incoming request, and, if applicable, with a copy of the requested report of examination.

Regulatory Risk Assessment

The OCC's primary supervisory focus, with respect to a bank's insurance activities, is assessing the material risks that those activities may pose to the national bank and the effectiveness of the bank's oversight systems for monitoring and controlling those risks. The bank's insurance activities can pose direct risks to the bank's earnings, capital, liquidity and reputation, if not properly managed. The risk assessment should consider the items discussed in the booklet sections, "Applicable Legal and Regulatory Requirements," "Risks," and "Risk Management Processes."

---

[10] Examiners can refer to the OCC Intranet (sitemap/legal/sharing agreements) for a list of states that have signed agreements with the OCC.

The OCC's risk assessment process is consistent with GLBA functional regulation requirements. Also, this business line risk assessment conforms to the OCC's supervision by risk approach and should be integrated into the bank's normal supervisory process for evaluating the bank's overall risk profile. The risk assessment process consists of a preliminary risk assessment that will determine whether the insurance activities pose a material risk to the bank and what, if any, additional supervisory efforts are warranted in making this risk determination. If additional supervisory efforts are necessary, the examiner selects the appropriate steps from the "Additional Risk Assessment" section. The risk assessment process anticipates that the OCC's examinations of an FRA or unaffiliated third-party insurance provider will be infrequent; nevertheless, the process does establish protocol in the event such an examination is considered.

The risk assessment of the bank's insurance activities generally will include a bank level evaluation of the nature of the activities, strategic plans, financial significance to the bank's earnings, capital and liquidity, risk management systems, and compliance with banking laws. OCC examiners should use sources, such as routine meetings with bank management, regular reviews of existing bank reports, information obtained from state insurance regulators, and any applicable OCC reports to aid in the development of the consolidated bank assessment of risk. OCC examiners should review and update data on the OCC's electronic information systems during the bank's normal supervisory cycle or as requested.

Refer to the "Risk Assessment Process" section for more guidance in conducting the risk assessment.

Applicable Legal and Regulatory Requirements

Potentially relevant statutory, regulatory, and OCC policy requirements may apply to a national bank when insurance activities are conducted through the bank, FRAs, or unaffiliated third parties. Examiners' risk assessments of insurance activities encompass evaluating national banks' risk management functions. This includes determining the effectiveness of banks' systems for ensuring compliance with applicable legal and regulatory requirements. Following is a summary of these requirements that add to the statutory provisions discussed in the "National Bank Insurance Powers" section.

Insurance Customer Protections - 12 CFR 14

National banks must comply with the OCC's insurance consumer protection rule published under 12 CFR 14, which implements section 305 of GLBA. This regulation applies to retail sales practices, solicitations, advertising, or offers of any insurance or annuity product by a depository institution or any person engaged in such activities at an office of the institution or on behalf of the institution. Refer to appendix B for a more detailed discussion of this regulation.

Privacy Rule - 12 CFR 40 and the Fair Credit Reporting Act

A national bank and its financial and operating subsidiaries that provide insurance to consumers must comply with the privacy provisions under Title V of GLBA. Pursuant to the requirements of GLBA, the OCC, the Federal Reserve Board, the Federal Deposit Insurance Corporation, and the Office of Thrift Supervision have issued an interagency rule that governs the privacy of consumers' nonpublic personal information. National banks are subject to the OCC's privacy rule. However, functionally regulated financial and operating subsidiaries that offer insurance to consumers are not covered by the OCC's privacy rule, but must comply with state privacy requirements.

The interagency privacy rule implements the provisions of GLBA that require each bank (and other types of financial institutions, including insurance agents and insurance underwriters) to notify its customers about the bank's privacy policies and to provide consumers with an opportunity to opt out of information sharing between the bank and certain nonaffiliated third parties. Similarly, a bank's insurance subsidiary would have to provide its customers with its own privacy and opt out notices, although the rule would permit a company-wide notice where it accurately reflects each institution's practices.

The rule requires that these privacy and opt out notices be provided to individual consumers who establish a customer relationship with the bank, generally not later than the time the customer relationship is established. Unless an exception applies, these notices also must be provided to any other consumer, even if not a "customer" of the bank, before the bank discloses that consumer's nonpublic personal information to a nonaffiliated third party.

While the privacy rule applies to the sharing of information by a bank with nonaffiliated third parties, affiliate sharing of certain consumer information is subject to the Fair Credit Reporting Act (FCRA). In general, if a bank wants to share with its insurance subsidiary information from a credit report or from a consumer application for credit (such as assets, income, or marital status), the bank must first notify the consumer about the intended sharing and give the consumer an opportunity to opt out of it. The same rules would apply to an insurance company that wants to share information from credit reports or from applications for insurance. Failure to provide notice and opt out may turn the bank or insurance company into a consumer reporting agency. Affiliate sharing notices should be included in the bank's or insurance company's privacy notice. More information on the FCRA and the privacy rule are provided in appendix C of this booklet.

Federal Prohibitions on Tying - 12 USC 1972

Tying the availability of credit from the bank to the purchase of insurance offered by the bank or a bank affiliate is illegal. Under 12 USC 1972, a bank is prohibited (subject to certain exceptions) from requiring a customer to obtain credit, property, or services as a prerequisite to obtaining other credit, property, or services. This standard applies whether the customer is retail or institutional, or the transaction is on bank premises or off. The OCC has extended these protections to cover national bank operating subsidiaries. See appendix D for more specifics on this rule.

Restrictions on Transactions with Affiliates - 12 USC 371c, 371c-1

A national bank is subject to certain quantitative and qualitative restrictions on transactions with affiliates as prescribed by sections 23A and 23B of the Federal Reserve Act, 12 USC 371c and 371c-1. These legal restrictions apply to transactions between a bank (or its subsidiaries) and affiliates conducting insurance activities. They also apply to transactions between a bank and its own financial subsidiary.

The principal requirements of 12 USC 371c are as follows. The statute provides that for any one affiliate, the aggregate amount of covered transactions may not exceed 10 percent of the bank's capital stock and surplus. For all affiliates, the aggregate amount of covered transactions may not exceed 20 percent of the bank's capital stock and surplus. In addition, an extension of credit to an affiliate and a guarantee, acceptance, or letter of credit issued on behalf of an affiliate, must meet specific collateral requirements. Further, under section 371c any covered transaction must be made on terms and conditions that are consistent with safe and sound banking practices. Section 371c also prohibits the purchase of low-quality assets by a bank (or its subsidiaries) from an affiliate. Generally low-quality assets are defined as substandard, doubtful, loss, other assets especially mentioned, or delinquent.

The principal requirement of 12 USC 371c-1 is that transactions covered by that statute must be on terms and under circumstances that are substantially the same, or at least as favorable to the bank, as those prevailing at the time for comparable transactions with or involving other nonaffiliated companies; or in the absence of comparable transactions, on terms and under circumstances that in good faith would be offered to or would apply to, nonaffiliated companies. Generally, this requirement means that the transactions must be conducted on an arm's-length basis, and the bank must receive at least fair market value for any assets it sells, or services it provides, to its affiliate.

A covered transaction under 12 USC 371c is an extension of credit to an affiliate; a purchase of, or investment in, affiliate securities; a purchase of assets from an affiliate; the acceptance of affiliate securities as collateral for a loan to any borrower; or the issuance of a guarantee, acceptance, or letter of credit on behalf of an affiliate. Transactions covered by 12 USC 371c-1 include covered transactions under 12 USC 371c, the sale of securities or other assets to an affiliate, including assets subject to an agreement to repurchase, and the payment of money or the furnishing of services to an affiliate under contract, lease, or otherwise.

Advisory Letter 96-8, "Guidance on Insurance and Annuity Sales Activities"

This booklet incorporates and retains certain standards from Advisory Letter 96-8 under the "Risk Management" section. Other portions of Advisory Letter 96-8 were superceded by GLBA's requirements on the applicability of state laws, customer privacy, and customer protections. Advisory Letter 96-8 is rescinded with the release of this booklet.

Risks

The OCC assesses banking risk relative to the potential that events, expected or unanticipated, may have an adverse effect on the bank's earnings and capital. The primary risks associated with insurance activities are transaction, compliance, strategic, reputation, and credit risk. Insurance underwriting and reinsurance may pose additional risks, such as mortality risk, adverse selection, excess capacity, and poor underwriting results that extend beyond the scope of this discussion. All of these risks can pose direct risks to the bank's franchise value if not managed properly. For example, inferior product delivery, ineffective controls, and poor planning can result in potential legal costs and loss of business. The following is a more detailed discussion of the primary risks associated with insurance activities.

Transaction Risk

Transaction risk is the risk to earnings or capital arising from fraud, error, and the inability to deliver products and services, maintain a competitive position, and manage information. Increasing or high transaction risk exists in a bank whose ability to transact business is impeded by inefficient operating systems or poor internal controls. Ineffective operating systems can result in poor product delivery, including unacceptable levels of errors and exceptions or general systems failures. Banks with low transaction risk typically have efficient delivery systems, including capable staffs, strong information systems and processing, viable backup systems, and appropriate insurance coverage for errors and omissions.

A bank's insurance activities, which may include the issuance of binders and policies, the forwarding of premiums, the filing of claims, and electronic product delivery, pose transaction risk to the bank if they are not performed efficiently and accurately. Transaction risk is elevated for banks that internally process premium payments and loss claims, including the potential liability for late or non-remittance of payments to the underwriter.

For insurance sales, underwriting, or reinsurance activities, examiners assess transaction risk by evaluating the adequacy of the bank's risk management over insurance application, processing, and delivery systems and controls. They consider the volume and type of policies issued, the capabilities of systems and technology in relation to current and prospective volume, contingency preparedness, and exposures through the claims and payment processing systems.

Compliance Risk

Compliance risk is the risk to earnings or capital arising from violations of or noncompliance with laws, rules, regulations, internal policies and procedures, or ethical standards. Compliance risk exposes a bank to the possible loss of business, fines, payment of damages, and voidance of contracts.

The regulatory framework for bank insurance activities is complex, consisting of both federal and state legal requirements. Banks, particularly those with multi-state programs, must research carefully and understand fully the compliance requirements for each state in which they conduct insurance activities. Moreover, this regulatory framework addresses both safety and soundness and consumer protection provisions. It is crucial that banks comply with all applicable regulatory requirements.

Banks without adequate policies, training, MIS, and audit/compliance programs are subject to high compliance risk, because of the lack of effective systems for self-regulating this business line. A pattern of complaints is a lagging indicator of compliance problems. Conversely, banks that clearly incorporate authority and responsibility into their risk management programs and develop strong compliance systems are likely to exhibit low compliance risk.

Examiners assess compliance risk by evaluating the comprehensiveness of a bank's compliance program relative to the complexity of the bank's insurance activities. Examiners should consider the volume and nature of complaints received, violations of law cited, and enforcement actions taken by banking and functional regulators, and the quality and effectiveness of the audit/compliance program.

Strategic Risk

Strategic risk is the risk to earnings or capital arising from adverse business decisions, improper implementation of decisions, or lack of responsiveness to industry changes. Strategic risk in insurance activities may be high in banks that, in an effort to remain competitive, rapidly and aggressively introduce new products and services without fully performing due diligence reviews or implementing the infrastructure to support the activity. A culture that focuses almost exclusively on production and income can motivate undesirable sales and underwriting practices if appropriate risk management systems are not in place. Conversely, banks with low strategic risk would likely exhibit a corporate culture that includes appropriate planning, due diligence, implementation, delivery networks, and risk management systems.

Management's knowledge of the economic dynamics and market conditions of the insurance industry, including the cost structure and profitability of each major insurance line, can help limit strategic risk. The bank's structure and managerial talent must support its strategies and degree of innovation in offering new or nontraditional products. Strategic risk may vary depending on whether the bank acquires an existing insurance agency, underwriter, or reinsurer with established systems and controls or starts a new one.

Examiners assess strategic risk by determining whether bank management: has performed adequate due diligence reviews of the insurance companies whose products will be offered, underwritten, or reinsured; evaluated the feasibility and profitability of each new insurance product and service before it is offered; and established appropriate systems and controls. Examiners will also assess the adequacy of the bank's infrastructure to support agency, underwriting, and reinsurance activities.

Reputation Risk

Reputation risk is the risk to earnings or capital arising from negative public opinion that can affect the bank's ability to establish new business and retain existing relationships. Reputation risk associated with insurance sales can arise from inappropriate sales recommendations, deficient underwriting and reinsurance practices, poor service, violations of law, or litigation. Also, adverse events surrounding the insurance companies whose products are sold or underwritten through the bank may increase reputation risk. Reputation risk can be minimized by appropriate implementation and policing of the bank's insurance activities, to include effective due diligence in selecting products and their providers, as well as adequate policies, procedures, training, audit, and management information systems.

Banks that are entering into or expanding insurance activities without acquiring the necessary expertise or implementing the necessary risk management systems may experience high or increasing reputation risk. A focus on production and an anxiety for income may motivate undesirable sales or underwriting practices without the necessary systems and controls. Inappropriate sales recommendations or deficient underwriting or reinsurance practices, and violations of law could subject the bank to significant reputation risk and litigation, including class-action lawsuits which can give rise to significant potential liability. Banks with low or stable reputation risk are typically those that exercise caution in introducing new insurance products and services, or those that have been in insurance activities for some time and expand their product line gradually and only after performing the appropriate due diligence review.

Examiners assess reputation risk by evaluating the quality of the bank's risk controls including the due diligence process and oversight functions for ensuring appropriate sales, underwriting, and reinsurance practices. Examiners should also consider any current or pending litigation and analyze customer complaint information.

Credit Risk

Credit risk is the risk to earnings or capital arising from an obligor's failure to meet the terms of any contract with the bank or to otherwise fail to perform as agreed. Credit risk is found in all activities for which success depends on counterparty, issuer, or borrower performance. Banks relying on third parties to facilitate their insurance activities are exposed to credit risk, if the vendor is unable to meet the contractual requirements. Credit risk exists in credit-related insurance sales, underwriting, and reinsurance activities, if the insurance carrier fails to honor a claim. The insurance carrier's claim paying ability depends on its financial strength and willingness to pay. In many credit-related insurance sales, the bank is named as the beneficiary to receive insurance proceeds for debt repayment in the event of the borrower's death, unemployment, or disability. If the insurance company fails to pay benefits under the credit-related policy, the bank's credit risk exposure increases as debt repayment becomes uncertain.

Banks involved in underwriting credit-related insurance and reinsurance are exposed to credit risk from the probability that claims will be presented for payment or will not be honored by another underwriter. The credit quality of the primary insurance company and duration of the contracts are key variables. Before establishing a relationship with a primary underwriter or a reinsurer, the bank should conduct an independent financial analysis and review the insurance carrier's ratings. Credit risk may be reduced partially by the support provided by state insurance guaranty associations or funds.

Examiners assess credit risk in the bank's insurance activities by evaluating the significance of exposures, loss experience, and controls over the associated activities. The examiner of insurance activities should coordinate with the examiner responsible for assessing credit underwriting standards when determining risk exposures.

Risk Management Processes

This section describes how national banks should manage the risks associated with insurance activities. The board and senior bank management should develop and implement effective risk management processes that effectively assess, control, and monitor the risks emanating from a bank's insurance activities. An effective risk management system is characterized by a board and senior management that are actively involved in the development and maintenance of effective supervision and sound risk management processes. Evaluating the effectiveness of the bank's risk management processes is a key component of the OCC's risk assessment.

Program Management Plan

A bank's board of directors is responsible for overseeing insurance activities conducted directly by the bank or through contractual arrangements with third parties, including bank subsidiaries, affiliates, or unaffiliated providers. In carrying out this responsibility, the board should adopt an appropriate program management plan to guide the bank's insurance activities. Aspects of the plan may be articulated in the bank's strategic plan for insurance activities or in other board-approved directives. The comprehensiveness of the plan should be commensurate with the complexity of the bank's insurance activities. This plan should articulate the board's risk tolerance and establish the necessary systems for controlling the program's risks. Annually, the board should reevaluate the plan for appropriateness and effect any necessary changes. At a minimum, the plan for insurance activities should address:

Program objectives, strategic direction, and risk tolerance standards. The board's plan should address the insurance program's objectives and establish the strategies for achieving them. The plan should describe the insurance program, including risks associated with the activities, and the board's risk tolerance levels.

Organizational structure and authority. The plan should establish the organizational structure for insurance activities and clearly delineate program authority, responsibility, and accountability. Depending upon the size of the bank, this structure may be an individual, a group of individuals, or a committee.

Policies and procedures. The plan should require establishing appropriate policies and procedures commensurate with the structure and complexity of insurance activities. These guidelines should ensure that the program's objectives are met without compromising customers' best interests.

Risk management system. The plan should reflect the board's commitment to risk management and a sound internal control system. It should outline a comprehensive risk management system that is appropriate for the bank's structure, complexity, and diversity of operations. A risk management function should include, as appropriate, senior managers, line managers, and personnel from compliance, audit, legal operations, human resources, information systems, and product development.

Management information systems (MIS). The plan should establish the appropriate MIS necessary for the board to oversee properly the bank's insurance activities. Board MIS should provide sufficient information to evaluate and measure the effect of actions taken. Also, the plan should provide for appropriate senior management MIS that may include sales volumes and trends, profitability, policy exceptions, customer complaints, and other data outlining compliance with laws and policies.

Bank Risk Assessment

The board and senior management should have processes in place to identify the risks associated with the bank's insurance activities. These processes should also determine how those risks will be measured and what controls and monitoring systems are needed. The bank should clarify the risk measurement and reporting processes it expects from bank managers and third-party providers.

Over time, risks may vary because of changes in the bank's strategies, product lines, personnel, or economic environment. The bank's risk assessment should adapt to the changes and adequately address the risks.

Internal and independent risk assessment should be comprehensive. Staff assigned to manage risk should identify the types of risk and estimate the levels of risk created by the bank's insurance activities. The assessment should consider the differences in bank direct activities and third-party relationships.

Risk Identification

Depending upon the size of the institution, a risk management function may have responsibility for identifying the risk in insurance activities. This function (or person in a smaller institution) should be independent and objective. When insurance activities are performed exclusively by third parties, bank management should ensure that the third-party activities are consistent with the bank's corporate strategic goals. The bank should identify the strategic purposes and risks associated with the third-party activity to ensure that the standards are consistent with those employed by the bank and to ensure that they are within the bank's risk tolerance levels.

Risk Measurement

Management must decide what measurement system is appropriate for gauging the risks in insurance activities. Models may be used in quantifying the risks. Management could incorporate insurance risks in existing models measuring credit and operational risks. A model is only as good as the quality of its data and the expertise of its users. The bank should continually assess and validate models used in this process. OCC Bulletin 2000-16, Risk Modeling, provides guidance on validating computer-based financial models. For third-party relationships, management should receive sufficient information and reports that allow for effective measurement of risk.

Risk Monitoring

For both third-party and bank direct activity, bank management should be accountable for understanding the insurance products offered and the sales process and for assuring compliance with insurance laws, regulations, and rules. A control self-assessment program should be implemented. This program should include identification of performance criteria, internal controls, reporting needs, and contractual requirements. The bank may want to use internal auditors, compliance officers, and legal counsel to help analyze the risks associated with third-party relationships and establish the necessary control and reporting structures.

Risk Controls

Risk controls, including policies, procedures, processes, and systems, are necessary to maintain risk at levels consistent with the bank's risk tolerance levels. The bank should have a comprehensive set of controls for managing the insurance related risks affecting the national bank.

Adequate Policies and Procedures

Policies and procedures should be developed and implemented that comprehensively address the bank's insurance activities. The level of detail contained in a bank's policies and procedures will depend on the structure and complexity of the bank's program. For example, an insurance program involving nationwide product distribution and heavy sales volumes will require more elaborate policies and procedures than a bank's program that is limited credit life insurance sales to its loan customers.

Effective Due Diligence Processes

A third-party provider (affiliated or unaffiliated) may perform many of a national bank's insurance activities. Before entering into a relationship with a third party, a bank should establish a comprehensive program for managing the relationship. The program should be documented and should include appropriate due diligence for selecting providers, products, and services, and ongoing oversight of the relationship. The relationship should be supported with binding written agreements, and bank counsel should review all contracts before entering into a third-party relationship. If the relationship is with a third-party provider that is an affiliate, the relationship must be consistent with the requirements of sections 23A and 23B of the Federal Reserve Act, 12 USC 371c and 371c-1.[11] Refer to OCC Bulletin 2001-47, "Risk Management Principles for Third-Party Relationships."

Processes for Identification and Selection of Third Parties

Selecting a competent and qualified third-party provider is essential to managing third-party risk. An effective due diligence process should be used to identify and select a third party that will help the bank achieve its strategic

---

[11] The requirements of sections 23A and 23B of the Federal Reserve Act, 12 USC 371c and 371c-1, are summarized under the "Restrictions on Transactions with Affiliates - 12 USC 371c, 371c-1" section of this handbook.

goals. The bank should obtain information, as appropriate, on the firm's investment and business approaches, professional resources, financial strength, historical performance, regulatory history, personnel turnover, and other relevant factors. The due diligence process normally will consider the following factors:

- Background. When the third party was established, its ownership and affiliation, the history of regulatory actions, personnel turnover, and other relevant factors.

- Financial strength. The provider's current, past and projected financial performance, financial audits, credit ratings and analyses issued by nationally recognized independent credit rating agencies.

- Experience. The provider's capability to render the necessary expertise, operational and technical support for the products and services under contract, and management depth and quality, and training support for all employees. Consider any subcontractors used and their effects on the prime provider's capabilities.

- Reputation. The provider's business reputation, complaint records and methods of resolving complaints, commission structure, product pricing, the payment of claims, and the current regulatory/litigation environment.

- Business strategies and goals. The provider's business strategies and goals and whether they complement the bank's philosophies and risk appetite. Consider the provider's human resource policies, customer service philosophies, policies for managing costs and improving efficiency, and ethics.

- Effectiveness of risk management processes. The provider's policies and procedures, diversification guidelines, concentration limits, internal compliance and audit programs, contingency planning and disaster control systems, and the internal control environment.

- Written plans. The provider's written business resumption, recovery, continuity, and contingency plans; and whether they meet the bank's expectations and requirements.

- Management information systems (MIS). The provider's MIS capability in meeting the bank's information needs in a timely and comprehensive manner. MIS should cover client data, sales activity, product performance, financial, compliance, and complaint information.

- Products and services. Whether the variety of offerings meet the bank's criteria for its client base, products' underlying insurance underwriters possess the financial strength for paying claims, and product pricing is reasonable compared with similar product offerings from other vendors. Bank management should review a sample of marketing materials, particularly those using the bank's name, to ensure materials are appropriate.

Guidelines for Written Contracts

Bank management should ensure that expectations and obligations of each party are clearly defined within a binding written agreement or contract with each third-party provider. The document should address the following issues:

- Scope of the relationship. The types of insurance products or services that will be provided, software support and maintenance, training of employees, and customer service guidelines.

- Activities provided.   Agency or other insurance related activities that will be provided and whether they will be conducted on or off bank premises. The contract should describe, as applicable, the terms governing the use of the bank's space, compensation, human resources, and equipment. When dual employees are used, responsibilities and duties should be articulated clearly.

- Expectations and responsibilities. The means for monitoring ongoing performance and measuring the success of the third-party arrangement, including compliance with legal requirements.

- Management information reports. The types, frequency, and materiality of management information reports expected by bank management.

- Compensation and costs. Full descriptions of compensation, fees, and calculations for services provided, including charges based upon the volume of activity and fees for special requests. The contract should state clearly who is responsible for paying legal, audit, and examination fees associated with the insurance activity. The cost and responsibility for purchasing and maintaining hardware and software should be addressed.

- Indemnification. Provisions that release the bank from any potential liability. Such provisions can reduce the likelihood that the bank will be held liable for claims citing negligence of the third party. The bank may also consider limiting the third party's liability. If so, management should determine whether the proposed limit is in proper proportion to the amount of loss the bank might experience from the third party's failure to perform.

- Insurance coverage. Requirements for insurance coverage. The third party should maintain adequate insurance, including appropriate errors and omissions coverage, and should notify the bank of material changes to coverage.

- Dispute resolution. The process (arbitration, mediation, etc.) for resolving problems between the bank and the third party.

- Default and termination. What constitutes default, identity of remedies, and allowance for opportunities to cure defaults. The contract should include a provision that enables the bank to terminate the contract upon reasonable notice and without penalty, in the event the OCC or another regulator formally objects to the third-party arrangement. The contract should state termination and notification requirements with timeframes to allow for the orderly conversion to another provider. It should also provide for timely return of the bank's data and other resources.

- Customer complaints. Identity of the person(s) responsible for responding to and resolving complaints. The third party should forward to the bank copies of any complaints it receives from the bank's customers and copies of all follow up correspondence on those complaints.

Guidelines for Qualifications and Training

Banks should have knowledgeable, experienced, and qualified personnel to ensure that insurance activities are carried out in a manner that provides customers with competitive products, sound advice, and accurate information. Personnel should be familiar with the bank's policies and procedures to ensure compliance with its internal guidelines and applicable legal requirements. Timely and regularly scheduled training can keep personnel aware of the latest innovations in financial products, changes in bank policies, and developments in applicable laws or regulations. To achieve these goals, management should:

- Clearly define responsibilities of personnel authorized to sell insurance products and the scope of the activities of any third party involved in the sales program.

- Verify that sales personnel are licensed and in good standing under applicable state and federal laws.

- Ascertain whether individuals have been subject to any disciplinary action.

- Ensure that continuing education requirements are met.

- Limit the involvement of tellers and individuals not qualified to sell insurance to directing customers to qualified personnel who can provide authoritative information.

For third-party relationships, the bank should ensure that the vendor has processes in place to meet qualification and training requirements.

Guidelines to Prevent Inappropriate Recommendations or Sales

Customers interested in purchasing insurance products may have particular needs based on their financial status, current insurance coverage, or other circumstances. Customers inexperienced in dealing with financial products, particularly those products involving an investment risk, may also require more detailed information about the products offered. Sales programs should have effective guidelines to prevent inappropriate recommendations or sales. For example, management should communicate clearly to its sales personnel that it is unacceptable to recommend and sell new or replacement insurance policies to customers on the basis of commissions to the seller rather than on the benefits of the policy. Such "twisting" is inappropriate and a violation of most states' laws.

For bank direct activities, the bank is responsible for day-to-day supervision of the sales practices and management including the appropriateness of products for each customer. In arrangements with third parties (bank subsidiaries, bank affiliates, and unaffiliated entities), the bank oversees the third party and ensures that the vendor has policies and procedures to prevent inappropriate recommendations and sales. Day-to-day supervision of third-party sales practices is the responsibility of the third party.

Appropriate Employee Compensation Programs

Incentive compensation is commonly used to sell insurance and may increase customer awareness of the availability of the products offered by a bank. The sales program should have a compensation structure in place that does not encourage inappropriate sales practices. Sales should reflect the customer's best interest and the policy's benefits, not the commission derived from the transaction. Management should communicate clearly to the bank's sales personnel that it is unacceptable to engage in high-pressure sales tactics, sell duplicative or unnecessary insurance, or recommend and sell new or replacement insurance policies to customers for reasons other than the customers' benefit. Sales personnel who engage in such practices should be penalized, either through the compensation program or by termination, as appropriate. The bank is responsible for day-to-day supervision of the bank's employee compensation programs. For third-party relationships (bank subsidiaries, bank affiliates, and unaffiliated entities), bank management should ensure that the vendor has policies and procedures in place to ensure that its employee compensation programs are appropriate.

Any performance-based compensation should be:

- Conformed to applicable legal requirements.

- Approved by appropriate legal counsel.

- Addressed in a governing document or contract. These documents should discuss formally the performance-based compensation, including the basis of calculation and circumstances under which the fees will or will not be payable.

Any bank employee referral program should meet applicable legal requirements. For example, under 12 CFR 14, certain bank employees, including tellers, may receive a one-time nominal fee of a fixed dollar amount for each customer referred for insurance products. The payment of this referral fee cannot depend on whether the referral results in a transaction.

Risk Monitoring

Risk monitoring is necessary to evaluate the performance of the bank's risk strategies and control processes over insurance activities. Bank management responsible for risk monitoring should perform frequent, independent reviews of compliance with risk policies, procedures, and control systems. Noncompliance with established policies and procedures should be addressed through fully documented corrective action plans and communicated to affected persons. The frequency of monitoring should be determined based on the nature, complexity, and diversity of insurance activities and operations.

Ongoing Oversight of Third-Party Relationships

After entering into an arrangement with a third party (bank subsidiary, bank affiliate and unaffiliated entities), management should monitor the third party's activities and performance. Management's oversight program should be documented properly to facilitate the monitoring and management of the risks associated with third-party relationships. Management should dedicate sufficient staff with the necessary expertise to oversee the third party. The extent of a bank's oversight activities will vary depending on the nature of the arrangement. At a minimum, the bank should monitor the third party's financial condition, its controls, and the quality of its service and support. The monitoring of these areas may include:

- Evaluation of the third party's financial condition. Perform a comprehensive financial analysis at least annually, and more often depending upon the complexity of the third-party arrangement. Significant relationships with third parties should require audited financial statements.

- Financial obligations to subcontractors. Ensure that the third party's obligations are met in a timely manner.

- Insurance coverage. Review adequacy of the third party's coverage.

- Review audit reports. Review audit (e.g., internal audits, external audits, security reviews) and examination reports, if available, and follow up on any deficiencies noted.

- Policies relating to internal controls and security. Ensure that these policies continue to meet the bank's minimum guidelines and contract requirements.

- On-site quality assurance reviews. Perform reviews, targeting adherence to specified policies and procedures, when practicable and necessary.

- Coordinated audits and reviews. Coordinate with user groups.

- Compliance. Review compliance with applicable banking laws, including consumer protection legal requirements.

- Third party's business resumption contingency planning and testing. Review to ensure that all bank services can be restored within an acceptable time. For many critical services, annual or more frequent tests of the contingency plan are typical. Review any results of those tests and ensure that recovery times meet bank requirements.

- Third-party personnel. Monitor changes in key personnel allocated to the bank.

- Reports documenting the third party's performance. Review service level agreements regularly. Determine whether contractual terms and conditions are being met, and whether any revisions to service-level agreements or other terms are needed.

- Performance problems. Document and follow up on performance problems in a timely manner.

- Bank's strategic plan and goals. Evaluate the third party's ongoing ability to support and enhance its strategic plan and goals.

- Training. Ensure that adequate training is provided to bank employees.

- Customer complaints on the products and services. Review those provided by the third party and any complaint information available from the OCC, and the resolution of those complaints.

- Customer satisfaction. Consider using mystery shopper, customer call-back, or other customer satisfaction programs.

- Periodic meetings with contract parties. Discuss performance and operational issues.

- Documentation and records maintenance. Document and maintain records on contract compliance, revision, and dispute resolution.

Customer Complaints

Even the most well-managed insurance program can be subject to customer complaints. Both customers and the bank will benefit, if the bank has an orderly process for assessing and addressing customer complaints and resolving compliance issues. A process that keeps track of customer complaints also helps the bank to identify and monitor any systemic problems in its sales program that could harm its franchise. This process should include maintaining records on the number, nature, and disposition of customer complaints received by a bank, subsidiary, or affiliated or unaffiliated third party.

Management should also ensure that an effective process exist through which it receives information about complaints or other concerns about the bank's insurance sales, so that it may implement corrective measures. The bank's systems must be sufficient to monitor compliance with its policies, applicable federal and state laws, and OCC guidance.

Compliance and Audit Programs

Banks should develop and implement policies and procedures that ensure that insurance activities are conducted in compliance with applicable laws and regulations, internal policies and procedures, and guidelines. Compliance procedures should also provide for a system to monitor customer complaints and their resolution. When applicable, compliance procedures should call for verification that third-party sales are being conducted in a manner consistent with the governing agreement with the bank.

Personnel performing the audit or compliance review of the bank's insurance activities should be qualified and should have the necessary expertise to perform the assigned tasks. Audit and compliance personnel should also engage in ongoing training to keep abreast of emerging developments in banking, securities, and insurance laws and regulations.

There should be an independent review of the insurance program. Independence may be established, if the audit or compliance personnel: determine the scope, frequency, and depth of their own reviews; report their findings directly to the board of directors or an appropriate committee of the board; have their performance evaluated by persons independent of the insurance activity; and receive compensation that is not connected to the success of insurance product sales.

An audit and compliance function is essential to effective risk management and internal control monitoring. Any deficiencies in internal controls and risk management processes should be addressed through written corrective action plans and monitored effectively for adequate follow-up and resolution.

The following risk assessment process is applicable when evaluating the risks of a national bank's insurance activities, whether conducted by the bank directly or through affiliated or unaffiliated third parties. The purpose of the review is to determine whether the bank's insurance activities pose a material risk to the bank. The review will normally be based on supervisory information obtained during routine meetings with bank risk managers or during regularly scheduled monitoring of bank information reports.

The risk assessment conforms to the OCC's supervision by risk approach and should be integrated into the normal supervisory process for evaluating the bank's overall risk profile. The risk assessment process consists of a preliminary risk assessment that will determine whether insurance activities pose a material risk to the bank and what, if any, additional supervisory efforts are warranted in making this risk determination. If additional supervisory efforts are necessary, the examiner selects the appropriate steps from the additional risk assessment process. The risk assessment process anticipates that the OCC's examinations of an FRA or unaffiliated third-party insurance provider will be infrequent; nevertheless, the process does establish protocol in the event the risk assessment indicates that such an examination may be needed. The process is detailed in the next three sections under "Preliminary Risk Assessment," "Additional Risk Assessment, " and "Risk Assessment Conclusions."

The risk assessment process is consistent with GLBA functional regulation requirements limiting the OCC's authority to obtain reports directly from and examine an FRA, unless certain conditions exist. If the risk assessment identifies potential significant risk to the bank from the FRA's insurance activities, the OCC will seek additional information or reports from the appropriate functional regulator. If such information or report is not made available, the OCC may seek to obtain it from the FRA, if the information or report is necessary to assess:

- A material risk to the affiliated national bank;

- Compliance with a federal law the OCC has specific jurisdiction to enforce with respect to the insurance entity; or

- The system for monitoring and controlling operational and financial risks that may pose a threat to the safety and soundness of the affiliated national bank.

These limitations do not restrict the OCC from seeking information on insurance activities conducted directly by the national bank, nor from obtaining information on an FRA from the bank or from sources other than the FRA to the extent needed to evaluate risks an FRA poses to the bank.

GLBA also limits the OCC's ability to directly examine insurance activities conducted by FRAs. The OCC may directly examine the FRA only when:

- There is reasonable cause to believe that the company is engaged in activities that pose a material risk to the affiliated national bank;

- After reviewing relevant reports, a reasonable determination is made that an examination of the company is necessary to adequately inform the OCC of the system for monitoring and controlling operational and financial risks that may pose a threat to the safety and soundness of the affiliated national bank; or

- Based on reports and other information available, there is reasonable cause to believe that the company is not in compliance with federal law that the OCC has specific jurisdiction to enforce against the company, including provisions relating to transactions with affiliates, and the OCC cannot make such determination through examination of the national bank.

Before an examiner requests information from or conducts an examination of an FRA or other unaffiliated third party, the examiner should discuss the circumstances with the appropriate deputy comptroller. Also, the examiner should consult the appropriate deputy comptroller before contacting the functional regulator for additional information on an FRA's or unaffiliated third party's insurance activities.

These examination limitations do not apply to insurance activities conducted directly by the bank. In these arrangements, the state insurance regulators and the OCC have joint jurisdiction. The state insurance regulator is responsible for functional regulation of the bank's insurance activities. The

OCC is responsible for supervising the safety and soundness of these activities and for evaluating compliance with banking law requirements.

These examination limitations also do not apply to unaffiliated bank service companies subject to the Bank Service Company Act (BSCA) that provide insurance or insurance-related services to a bank. The OCC will continue to examine bank service companies consistent with the OCC's authority under the BSCA, 12 USC 1861 through 12 USC 1867. The OCC's supervisory focus in these examinations is on the bank service company's effect on the bank's safety and soundness.

The preliminary risk assessment should conform to the OCC's supervision by risk approach and should be integrated into the normal supervisory process. The preliminary risk assessment should be used to determine whether the national bank's insurance activities conducted in the bank, an FRA, or an unaffiliated third party pose a material risk to the bank. The preliminary risk assessment will also determine what, if any, additional supervisory efforts are warranted in making the risk determination.

Step 1: Develop a preliminary assessment of the level and types of risks posed to a national bank by insurance activities conducted by the bank, an FRA, or an unaffiliated third party. This risk assessment should determine whether the activities pose material risk to the bank. This assessment will be used in deciding whether additional supervisory efforts are necessary and, if appropriate, to establish the scope of the additional risk assessment.

1.   Review the related findings in the OCC's electronic information systems that were prepared during the last supervisory cycle.

2.   Contact the OCC's Customer Assistance Group to obtain any insurance related complaints (1-800-613-6743 or customer.assistance @occ.treas.gov).

3.   If appropriate and necessary, obtain from the bank the following information and reports applicable to insurance activities:

   ❑ Board of director minutes and information reports.
   ❑ Oversight committee minutes and information reports.
   ❑ Risk management information reports.
   ❑ Compliance and audit program reports.
   ❑ Fiscal and interim financial reports.
   ❑ Litigation reports.
   ❑ Client complaint information.

4.   Discuss the following with the bank's risk managers.

   • Significant risk issues and management strategies relating to insurance activities.
   • Significant changes in strategies, services, and distribution channels.

- Significant changes in organization, policies, controls, and information systems.
- External factors affecting insurance activities and strategies to address these issues.

5. Develop a preliminary risk assessment and discuss it with the bank examiner-in-charge (EIC) for perspective and strategy coordination. Consider:

- The nature of the bank's insurance activities. In general, agent activities present less risk to the bank than underwriting.

- The bank's strategic plan for its insurance activities.

- The significance of current and planned earnings from insurance activities relative to the bank's earnings.

- The sensitivity of insurance revenues relative to changing market or other external conditions.

- The amount of capital necessary to support insurance activities.

- The impact on the bank's liquidity from insurance activities either through direct funding requirements or from reputation risk.

- Information obtained from the OCC's electronic information systems.

- Any risk management deficiencies identified previously by the OCC, functional regulators, or the bank's risk control functions.

Also consider the following examples of insurance activities that involve potentially higher risks:

- Aggressive strategic plans and actions for expansion through acquisitions, mergers, and alliances.

- Significant program expansions by increasing product lines, licensing more agents, using more aggressive and varied distribution networks, and broadening the geographic target market.

- Sales programs involving riskier lines of business or significant concentrations of business.

- Underwriting activities.

- Manufacturing and marketing proprietary products.

- Deficiencies in the bank's oversight supervision and risk management systems.

- Negative findings from insurance regulators, auditors, compliance or risk managers.

- Adverse publicity or significant litigation.

Step 2: Determine whether the preliminary risk assessment is sufficient in assessing:

- Materiality of the risks posed to the bank from insurance activities.

- Effectiveness of the bank's risk management systems.

- Compliance with legal requirements under the OCC's jurisdiction.

1.   If the preliminary risk assessment is sufficient in evaluating the bank's risks, risk management, and compliance associated with insurance activities, and the aggregate risk is not material, the examiner should STOP and proceed to the steps under the "Risk Assessment Conclusions" section.

2.   If the preliminary risk assessment is insufficient in evaluating the bank's risks, risk management, and compliance associated with insurance activities, or the preliminary risk assessment indicates aggregate risk is potentially material, the examiner should continue with Step 3 for guidance on performing an additional risk assessment of the bank.

Step 3: Establish the objectives, scope, and work plans for the additional risk assessment of the bank to be completed during the supervisory cycle.

1. Based on the preliminary risk assessment, and in consultation with the bank EIC, prepare and submit a final planning memorandum for approval by the bank EIC that includes:

   • A preliminary business and risk assessment profile of insurance activities.

   • The objectives for the additional risk assessment.

   • The timing and projected workdays for the additional risk assessment.

   • The scope of the additional risk assessment to be completed. The selected steps should be consistent with the indications of risk identified during the preliminary risk assessment and focus on the identification of material risk to the bank from insurance activities. The steps to be used in this assessment should be selected from among those provided in the "Additional Risk Assessment" section.

   • Required examiner resources to complete the additional risk assessment.

   • The types of communication planned, such as meetings and final written products.

2. Complete the following after receiving EIC approval of the planning memorandum:

   • Select the examiner staff and make assignments consistent with the objectives, scope, and time frames of the planned additional risk assessment.

   • Discuss the risk assessment plan with appropriate bank personnel and make suitable arrangements for on-site national bank accommodations and additional information requests.

   • Contact each member of the examiner staff and provide necessary details concerning schedules and assignment responsibilities.

   • Consult closely with, and obtain authorization from, the bank EIC before completing the additional risk assessment.

Note: If necessary, refer to the "Examination Planning and Control," "Large Bank Supervision," and "Community Bank Supervision" booklets of the Comptroller's Handbook for additional information on planning these risk assessments.

This additional risk assessment should be used when:

1.   The preliminary risk assessment is insufficient in evaluating the bank's risks, risk management, and compliance associated with insurance activities conducted in the bank, an FRA, or an unaffiliated third party, or

2.   The preliminary risk assessment indicates aggregate risk is potentially material.

The selected steps should be consistent with the indications of risk identified during the preliminary risk assessment and should focus on the identification of material risk to the bank from insurance activities.

Examiners should consult and obtain authorization from the bank EIC before completing the additional risk assessments.

Quantity of Risk Assessment

Transaction Risk

Step 1: Identify and estimate the quantity of transaction risk posed to the bank from insurance activities.

1.   Analyze bank information reports relating to transaction processing and reporting in insurance activities. Consider the following structural assessment factors:

- The volume, type, and complexity of transactions, products, and services offered through the insurance program. Determine whether the bank insurance unit internally processes premiums and claims.

- The condition, security, capacity, and recoverability of systems.

- The complexity and volume of conversions, integrations, and system changes.

- The development of new markets, products, services, technology, and delivery systems to maintain a competitive position or gain strategic advantage.

- The volume and severity of operational, administrative, and accounting control exceptions and losses from fraud and operating errors.

2. Analyze and discuss with appropriate bank risk managers how the following strategic assessment factors affect the quantity of transaction risk in insurance activities:

- The impact of strategic factors, including marketing plans and the development of new markets, products, services, technology, and delivery systems.

- The impact of acquisition and divestiture strategies.

- The maintenance of an appropriate balance between technology innovation and secure operations.

3. Analyze and discuss with appropriate bank risk managers how the following external assessment factors affect the quantity of transaction risk in insurance activities:

- The effect of external factors including economic, industry, competitive, and market conditions; legislative and regulatory changes; and technological advancement.

- The effect of infrastructure threats on the bank's ability to deliver timely support and service.

- The ability of service providers to provide and maintain service level performance that meets the requirements of the insurance activities.

4. Obtain the results of the bank information systems examination activities. Analyze and discuss the conclusions and recommendations with the assigned examiner(s) as they relate to insurance activities.

Step 2: Reach a conclusion on the quantity of transaction risk posed to the bank from insurance activities.

Compliance Risk

Step 1: Identify and estimate the quantity of compliance risk posed to the bank from insurance activities.

1. Obtain and analyze the type and level of policy exceptions, internal control deficiencies, and law violations that have been identified and reported internally by the bank. Review information from the following sources:

    ❑ Board and committee minutes and reports.
    ❑ Risk management division reports.
    ❑ Compliance reports.
    ❑ Control self-assessment reports.
    ❑ Internal and external audit reports.
    ❑ Regulatory reports.
    ❑ Other OCC examination programs.

2. Obtain and analyze the type and volume of litigation and consumer complaints related to insurance activities.

3. Discuss significant litigation and complaints with the appropriate bank risk managers to determine the risk to capital and the appropriateness of corrective action and follow-up processes. Refer to the "Litigation and Other Legal Matters" booklet of the Comptroller's Handbook for additional procedures, if necessary.

Step 2: Refer to appendix B, "Insurance Customer Protections," for examination procedures to review compliance with 12 CFR 14. These procedures can be used when, in the examiner's judgment, they are necessary to determine the level of compliance or the quality of the bank's compliance program, or when the OCC has identified or suspects violations.

Step 3: Determine whether the bank is in compliance with the legal requirements on transactions with affiliates under sections 23A and 23B of the Federal Reserve Act, 12 USC 371c and 371c-1.

Step 4: Reach a conclusion on the quantity of compliance risk posed to the bank from insurance activities. If applicable, consider the following assessment factors:

- The nature and extent of business activities, including new products and services.

- The volume and significance of noncompliance with policies and procedures, laws, regulations, prescribed practices, and ethical standards.

- The amount and significance of litigation and customer complaints.

Strategic Risk

Step 1: Identify and estimate strategic risk posed to the bank from insurance activities.

1. Analyze the bank's strategic plan for insurance activities by considering the following assessment factors.

   - The magnitude of change in established corporate mission, goals, culture, values, or risk tolerance.

   - The financial objectives as they relate to the short- and long-term goals of the bank.

   - The market situation, including product, customer demographics, and geographic position.

   - Diversification by product, geography, and customer demographics.

   - Past performance in offering new products and services.

   - Risks and performance in implementing innovative or unproven products, services, or technologies.

   - Merger, acquisition and alliance plans, opportunities, and past experience.

- Potential or planned entrance into new businesses, product lines, or delivery channels, or implementation of new systems.

2. Discuss the strategic plan with appropriate bank risk managers and assess the impact of external factors on strategic risk. Consider:

- Economic, industry, and market conditions (impact on projected revenue).

- Legislative and regulatory change.

- Technological advances.

- Competition.

Step 2: Reach a conclusion on the quantity of strategic risk posed to the bank from insurance activities.

Reputation Risk

Step 1: Identify and estimate reputation risk posed to the bank from insurance activities.

1. Discuss with appropriate bank risk managers the affect of the following assessment factors on reputation risk from insurance activities:

- The volume and types of insurance activities.

- Merger and acquisition plans and opportunities.

- Potential or planned entrance into new businesses, product lines, or technologies (including new delivery channels), particularly those that may test legal boundaries.

2. Discuss with appropriate risk managers the affect of the following external factors on reputation risk from insurance activities:

- The market's or public's perception of the corporate mission, culture, and risk tolerance of the bank and the insurance activities.

- The market's or public's perception of the bank's and the insurance entity's financial stability.

- The market's or public's perception of the quality of products and services offered by the bank and the insurance entity.

- The impact of economic, industry, and market conditions; legislative and regulatory change; technological advances; and competition.

Step 2: Reach a conclusion on the quantity of reputation risk posed to the bank from insurance activities.

Credit Risk

Step 1: Identify and estimate credit risk posed to the bank from insurance activities.

1.   Obtain and analyze bank information relating to credit exposures in insurance activities. The focus is on the bank's credit-related insurance, underwriting, and reinsurance activities. Consider the following risk assessment factors:

   - Volume and trends in the book of business.
   - Significant concentrations in the book of business, including individual, industry, geographic, and product concentrations.
   - Financial strength and claims payment ability of counterparties.
   - Loss experience and anticipated losses.
   - Adequacy of the bank's allowance for loan and lease losses.
   - Duration of insurance contracts.
   - Expertise and experience of personnel responsible for overseeing and managing credit risk.
   - Economic and other external factors.
   - Findings from the latest examination conducted by the state insurance regulators.

2.   Analyze the effectiveness of the bank's due diligence process for selecting and ongoing monitoring of insurance carriers involved in the bank's credit-related, underwriting, and reinsurance activities. Coordinate this effort with the applicable steps under the "Quality of Risk Management Process" section.

3.   Coordinate your analysis with the examiner responsible for credit underwriting risk.

Step 2: Reach a conclusion on the quantity of credit risk posed to the bank from insurance activities. If the bank is involved in reinsurance activities, continue to Step 3 for additional guidance.

Step 3: Perform additional analysis on the credit risk associated with the bank's reinsurance activities by understanding more about the nature of the bank's reinsurance business. Refer to the booklet's appendix A, "Insurance Product Types," for more information on reinsurance.

1.   Determine the method(s) used for ceding risks in the bank's reinsurance business and the proportion of the methods relative to the reinsurance activities. Consider:

   • Treaty reinsurance contracts require the reinsurer to underwrite part or all of a ceding company's book of business for one or more specific classes of business. Generally the reinsurer is bound automatically to reinsure any business the ceding company writes within these specific classes resulting in potentially greater risk than the method described next.

   • Facultative reinsurance contracts only require the reinsurer to underwrite individual policies of the ceding company rather than all risks within a particular class of business.

2.   Determine the loss basis structure of treaty and facultative reinsurance contracts. Consider whether the reinsurance activities operate under proportional or non-proportional agreements.

   • For proportional based reinsurance, consider whether the agreement involves quota share or surplus share arrangements.

   • Under quota share agreements, determine the percentage basis assumed in the bank's reinsurance business.

   • Under the surplus share agreements, determine the share proportion of the individual risk reinsured.

- For non-proportional (or excess of loss) agreements, identify the reinsurer's obligation to the primary insurer that is a predetermined amount of risk above the primary insurer's risk retention amount.

3. Determine whether the bank's reinsurance business uses retrocessions in transferring risk. If retrocessions are used, determine the level of coverage obtained and the effectiveness of reducing the reinsurance loss exposures.

Step 4: Reach a conclusion on the quantity of credit risk posed to the bank from reinsurance activities.

Policy

Step 1: Determine the adequacy and effectiveness of policies applicable to insurance activities.

1. Obtain the bank board's program management plan for insurance activities. Portions of this plan may be contained within the bank's strategic plan for insurance activities or in other board directives.

2. Review the program management plan to determine whether it is appropriate in guiding the bank's insurance activities. Determine whether the plan:

   - Was formally adopted by the board and receives annual board review and approval.

   - Establishes program objectives, strategic direction and risk tolerance standards.

   - Addresses organizational structure and authority.

   - Requires establishing appropriate policies and procedures.

   - Outlines a comprehensive risk management system appropriate for the bank's insurance activities.

   - Sets forth management information systems necessary for the board to oversee the activities properly.

3. Review policy documents and determine whether they:

   - Are approved formally by the board, or a designated committee(s).

   - Outline the program's goals and objectives, responsibilities, ethical culture, risk tolerance standards, and risk management framework consistent with the program management plan.

   - Address applicable law.

- Address all significant products and services, including:

  - Product offering criteria.
  - A list and description of insurance products and services.
  - Compensation schedules.
  - Descriptions of marketing and distribution channels.
  - How new products and services are developed and approved.

- Address the organizational structure and supervisory framework by establishing:

  - Organizational and functional charts.
  - Defined lines of authority and responsibility.
  - Delegation authority and approval processes.
  - Processes to select, employ, and evaluate legal counsel.
  - Standards for dealings with affiliated organizations.
  - Personnel practices.

- Establish appropriate information reporting and risk monitoring processes that include:

  - Initial and ongoing due diligence reviews of third-party vendor, products, and services.
  - Written contracts with vendors.
  - Proper oversight of bank direct programs.
  - Customer complaint resolution procedures.
  - Risk management systems.
  - Policy exception tracking and reporting processes.

- Address information systems and technology applications, such as:

  - Accounting and other transaction recordkeeping systems.
  - Management information system requirements.
  - Systems security and disaster contingency plans.

- Establish a compliance program. Determine whether the policy includes:

- A description of the program's purpose, responsibility, and accountability.
- Operating and testing procedures.
- Reporting and follow-up requirements and processes.
- Educational material and resource references.

4. Evaluate the policy review process and determine whether changes in risk tolerance, strategic direction, products and services, or the external environment are reviewed adequately and effectively.

5. Through discussion with management and other examiners, identify parts of the policy requiring development or revision. Consider:

- Recently developed and distributed products and services.
- Discontinued products, services, organizational structures, and information systems.
- Recent updates or revisions to existing policies and procedures.

Step 2: Draw a conclusion about the adequacy and effectiveness of the bank's risk management policies relating to insurance activities.

Processes

Step 1: Determine the adequacy and effectiveness of supervision by the bank's board and senior management.

1. Determine how supervisory oversight of insurance activities is organized and whether clear lines of authority, responsibility, and accountability are established through all levels of the organization. Obtain and evaluate:

- Bank bylaws and resolutions.
- Strategic plan and business strategies, including those related to functionally regulated entities.
- Board and management committees, charters, minutes, and reports.
- Management structures, authorities, and responsibilities.
- Other organizational structures.

2. If the board has delegated insurance supervisory oversight to one or more committees, review each committee's composition, charter,

meeting frequency, attendance, information reports, and board reporting processes for consistency with board guidance and regulatory requirements.

3. Evaluate the bank's strategic planning process for insurance activities focusing on whether this planning process:

- Is part of the bank's overall strategic and financial planning processes.

- Considers all significant elements of risk that affect the insurance program, such as internal risk tolerance standards, the corporate ethical culture, available financial resources, management expertise, technology capabilities, operating systems, competition, economic and market conditions, and legal and regulatory issues.

- Evaluates and determines the amount of capital necessary to support the business.

- Includes monitoring how well the insurance program implements the strategic plan and reports performance to the bank's board or the designated oversight body.

4. Evaluate the appropriateness of board and senior management reports for overseeing the bank's insurance activities.

5. Evaluate the effectiveness of the bank's initial due diligence process when identifying and selecting an affiliated or unaffiliated third-party provider. Refer to the "Identification and Selection of Third Parties" under the "Risk Control" section of this booklet for factors to consider in the selection process.

6. Evaluate the adequacy of the process used when establishing arrangements with affiliated and unaffiliated third-party providers. Refer to the "Guidelines for Written Contracts" under the "Risk Control" section of this booklet for factors to consider when entering into a formal arrangement.

7. Evaluate management's effectiveness in overseeing and monitoring relationships with affiliated and unaffiliated third parties. Refer to the

"Ongoing Oversight of Third Party Relationships" under the "Risk Monitoring" section of this booklet for factors to consider.

8.   Evaluate the effectiveness of management's supervision of bank direct insurance programs ensuring that risks are controlled appropriately.

Step 2: Reach a conclusion on the effectiveness of the bank's processes for managing risk posed to the bank from insurance activities.

Personnel

Step 1: Determine the adequacy and effectiveness of the bank's personnel policies, practices, and programs relating to insurance activities.

1.   Determine whether lines of authority and individual duties and responsibilities are defined and communicated clearly.

2.   Evaluate the bank's recruitment and employee retention program by reviewing:

- Recent success in hiring and retaining high-quality personnel.
- Level and trends of staff turnover, particularly in key positions.
- The quality and reasonableness of management succession plans.

3.   Analyze insurance activities compensation and performance evaluation program by considering whether:

- The compensation and performance evaluation program is appropriate for the types of products and services offered. Assess whether the compensation program provides incentive for improper sales practices.

- The program is formalized and reviewed periodically by the board and senior management.

- The program is consistent with the bank's risk tolerance and ethical standards.

- Responsibilities and accountability standards are clearly established for the performance evaluation program.

- The bank employee compensation program for insurance referrals conforms to legal requirements.

4. For bank direct insurance activities also evaluate the effectiveness of management's efforts in ensuring that sales personnel are qualified, properly trained, and receive appropriate supervision for their sales practices and other activities. For third-party relationships (bank subsidiary, affiliated and unaffiliated), evaluate the bank's oversight of the vendor's processes to meet qualification and training requirements.

5. Review the risk management training program by considering:

    - The types and frequency of training and whether the program is adequate and effective.

    - The adequacy of financial resources allocated to risk management training.

    - Whether employee training needs and accomplishments are a component of the performance evaluation program.

Step 2: Reach a conclusion on the effectiveness of the bank's personnel policies, practices, and programs relating to insurance activities.

Control Systems

Step 1: Determine the adequacy and effectiveness of the bank's control and monitoring systems relating to insurance activities.

1. Determine and evaluate the types of control and monitoring systems used by the bank's board and senior management. Consider:

    - Board and senior management risk monitoring processes.
    - Risk management groups.
    - Committee structures and responsibilities.
    - Management information systems.
    - Quantitative risk measurement systems.
    - Compliance programs.
    - Control self-assessment processes.

- Complaint resolution process.
- Audit program.

2. Determine the extent to which the bank's board and senior management are involved in supervising insurance activities. Consider:

   - Types and frequency of board and senior management reviews used to determine adherence to policies, operating procedures, and strategic initiatives, including those related to functionally regulated entities.

   - Adequacy, timeliness, and distribution of management information reports.

   - Responsiveness to risk control deficiencies and effectiveness of corrective action and follow-up activities.

3. If the bank has a separate risk management function responsible for insurance activities, review its purpose, structure, reporting process, and effectiveness. Consider:

   - Size, complexity, strategic plans, and trends in insurance activities.

   - Independence and objectivity.

   - Quality and quantity of personnel.

   - Quality of risk assessment, transaction testing, monitoring systems, and reporting processes.

4. Evaluate the bank's compliance program for insurance activities. Consider:

   - Extent of board and senior management commitment and support.

   - Line management responsibility and accountability.

   - Formalization, transaction testing, reporting structures, and follow-up processes.

- Qualifications and performance of compliance officer and supporting personnel.

- Communication systems.

- Training programs.

5. If the bank has implemented a control self-assessment program, obtain and evaluate information on the control self-assessments performed on insurance activities.

6. Obtain the latest internal and external audit reports and follow-up reports pertaining to insurance activities.

    - Determine the adequacy and effectiveness of the internal and external audit work on insurance activities by considering:

        - The independence, qualifications and competency of audit staff.
        - The timing, scope, and results of audit activity.
        - The quality of audit reports, work papers (if reviewed), and follow-up processes.

    - If the review of audit reports and work papers raises questions about audit effectiveness, discuss the issues with appropriate examiners and determine whether the scope of the audit review should be expanded. Issues that might require an expanded scope include:

        - Unexplained or unexpected changes in auditors or significant changes in the audit program.
        - Inadequate scope of the insurance activities audit program.
        - Deficient audit work papers or work papers that do not support audit conclusions.
        - Inadequate coverage of high risk insurance activities.
        - Inappropriate actions by insiders to influence the findings or scope of audits.

Step 2: Draw conclusions about the adequacy and effectiveness of the bank's control systems for managing risk posed to the bank from insurance activities. Forward the findings and recommendations, if applicable, to the examiner responsible for evaluating the bank's risk management, compliance, and audit programs.

Insurance Activities Risk Assessment Conclusions

These risk assessment conclusions should be used when completing both preliminary and additional risk assessments on the bank's insurance activities conducted in the bank, an FRA, or an unaffiliated third party.

Step 1: Reach a conclusion on the risks posed by insurance activities on the bank's consolidated risk profile.

1. Address the following in making this conclusion:

    - Materiality of the risks posed to the bank from insurance activities.
    - The effectiveness of the bank's risk management systems for controlling risks posed to the bank from insurance activities.
    - The bank's compliance with federal laws that the OCC has specific jurisdiction to enforce, including provisions relating to transactions between affiliates and the national bank.

2. Complete the large bank or community bank Risk Assessment System (RAS).

Step 2: Prepare a summary document that includes the conclusions under Step 1 and, if applicable, any other findings and recommendations for bank management.

Step 3: Discuss the review's findings with the bank EIC and adjust findings and recommendations as needed. Based on those results, determine the appropriate next steps with the bank EIC.

1. The examiner, with concurrence of the bank EIC, should proceed to Step 4 if the preliminary or additional risk assessments conclude that the bank is not exposed to material risk from insurance activities and further supervisory efforts are not warranted.

2. The bank EIC should STOP the assessment and discuss the circumstances with the appropriate deputy comptroller, if the preliminary or additional risk assessments conclude that the bank is exposed to material risk from insurance activities and additional information is needed from the FRA or unaffiliated third party; or an examination of the FRA or unaffiliated party is necessary; or

assessment findings should be referred to the functional regulators. Jointly, the bank EIC and the deputy comptroller should determine the appropriate next steps.

The bank EIC should have the following information available to discuss with the deputy comptroller:

- Summary document prepared in Step 2.

- The identity of the functional regulator and the name, address, and telephone number of the primary contact at the functional regulator (if applicable).

- A detailed description of the information to be requested or the reason(s) for requesting the information or for conducting the examination activity consistent with GLBA requirements, plus a copy of the proposed request to be delivered to the functional regulator.

Step 4: Hold a meeting with appropriate bank oversight committees or the appropriate risk managers to communicate the review's conclusions and recommendations, if appropriate, and authorized by the bank EIC. Allow management sufficient time before the meeting to review draft review conclusions and report comments.

Step 5: Prepare appropriate comments for a conclusion memorandum. Supplement the conclusion memorandum, when appropriate, to include:

- The objectives and scope of completed supervisory activities.

- Reasons for changes in the supervisory strategy, if applicable.

- Overall conclusions, recommendations for corrective action, and management commitments and time frames.

- Comments on any recommended administrative actions, enforcement actions, and civil money penalty referrals, if appropriate.

Step 6: Prepare final comments for the bank report of examination as requested by the EIC. The EIC may ask that these comments be presented on a separate report page. Perform a final check to determine whether the comments:

- Meet OCC report of examination guidelines.
- Support review conclusions and recommendations.
- Contain accurate violation citations.

Step 7: Update OCC electronic information systems, as requested, which may include:

- Matters requiring attention (MRA).
- RAS.
- Violations of law or regulation.
- Core knowledge database.

Step 8: Prepare a recommended supervisory strategy for the subsequent supervisory cycle and provide it to the EIC for review and approval.

Step 9: Prepare a memorandum or update work programs with any information that will facilitate future risk assessments or examinations.

Step 10: Organize and reference work papers in accordance with OCC guidelines.

Step 11: Complete and distribute assignment evaluations for assisting examiners.

Insurance Product Types

The following are the most common types of insurance sold in most states by licensed agents. However, many varieties of these products, as well as other products, are available through insurance companies. Therefore, examiners need to understand that, because products vary significantly in purpose and complexity, the selling agents need different knowledge, qualifications, and expertise. This discussion also includes reinsurance activities.

Credit Life and Other Credit-Related Insurance

Credit Life Insurance

Credit life insurance is the mainstay product in the bank insurance industry and has been sold by national banks for decades. Credit life insurance includes credit life, health and accident insurance, sometimes referred to as credit life and disability insurance, and mortgage life and disability insurance. These policies are issued on the life of the debtor and pay off consumer debt if the borrower dies or becomes disabled or unemployed before repayment. Mortgage life, disability, and unemployment policies make payments for a specified period of time or provide for a lump-sum payment, depending on the terms of the contract.

The OCC's regulation governing credit life insurance and the disposition of credit life insurance income is 12 CFR 2. This regulation sets forth the principles and standards that apply to a national bank's sales of credit life insurance and the limitations that apply to the receipt of income from those sales by certain individuals and entities associated with the bank. Additionally, banks must comply with certain disclosure requirements in connection with the sales of credit life insurance. These requirements are discussed further in 12 CFR 14 (see appendix B) and in the "Truth in Lending" booklet of the Comptroller's Handbook — Consumer Compliance Examinations.

Crop Insurance

Crop insurance, which includes both multiple peril crop insurance and hail/fire insurance, gives farmers a financial risk management tool to protect against excessive losses from crop failures or low yields. Historically, the federal government provided subsidies and price supports to the agriculture industry as a "safety net" to reduce the inherent production and price risk for the producer. Some minimal catastrophic coverage was required to participate in these programs. However, these programs, including federal crop insurance, were phased out under the Federal Agricultural Improvement and Reform Act of 1996. The void is being filled by crop insurance policies that are underwritten by private insurance companies.

Flood Insurance

The OCC issued 12 CFR 22 to implement the requirements of the National Flood Insurance Act of 1968 and the Flood Disaster Protection Act of 1973. The regulation addresses requirements to purchase flood insurance where available, exemptions, escrow requirement, required use of standard flood hazard determination form, force placement of insurance coverage, determination fees, notice of special flood hazards and availability of federal disaster relief assistance, and notice of servicer's identity.

A national bank is permitted to force place flood insurance if insurance is required by law and loan collateral is not covered by flood insurance or is covered in an amount less than that required by OCC's regulation. If a borrower fails to obtain flood insurance within 45 days after notification, the bank must purchase insurance on the borrower's behalf. The bank may charge the borrower for the cost of premiums and fees incurred in purchasing the insurance. Force placed flood insurance is not subject to the requirements of 12 CFR 14.

Life Insurance

The function of life insurance is to create a principal sum or estate, either through the death of the insured or through the accumulation of funds set aside for investment purposes. It is most commonly used to protect a person and his or her dependents against the undesirable financial consequences of premature death. Life insurance can be categorized into two broad types, temporary (term) and permanent insurance. There are numerous variations of these products. However, life insurance products generally fall within one or a combination of the following categories.

Term Life Insurance

Term life insurance is a basic type of insurance that offers death benefits only and generally has no cash value or savings element. Because term insurance provides only mortality protection, it provides the most coverage per premium dollar. However, premiums generally increase with the age of the policyholder. Most term life insurance policies are renewable for certain periods or until the policyholder attains a specified age. Additionally, many are convertible to permanent life insurance without the insured having to show evidence of insurability. Term life insurance is commonly used in conjunction with a home mortgage, in which case the beneficiary is usually a family member, not the lienholder.

Permanent Life Insurance

Whole Life
The cash value (essentially a savings account) of a whole life insurance policy, accrues according to a guaranteed, predetermined rate of return by the insurance company. These policies are also referred to as "general account" products because the general assets of the life insurance company support the cash value. Most types provide lifetime protection to age 100. If the insured is still living at that age, the policy "endows," and the guaranteed cash value equals the face amount of the policy. Also, cash value can be borrowed under the policy's loan provisions. Premiums and death benefits are guaranteed for the duration of the policy. Because premiums are constant, the cost is much higher in the early years than equal coverage under a term life insurance policy. However, the cost relationship reverses in later years as the cost of term life insurance rises with the age of the insured.

Combination Policies
Combination policies usually combine term insurance with a base whole life policy by using an attachment or rider. This combination provides for additional death benefits without a significant increase in premium cost.

Universal Life
Another form of permanent life insurance, universal life is an interest-sensitive form of life insurance, designed to provide flexibility in premium payments and death benefit protection. Policyholders can adjust the premiums, cash

values, and level of protection, subject to certain limitations, over the life of the contract. Additionally, unlike whole life, the interest credited to the cash value of universal life policies is based upon current interest rates, subject to an interest rate floor. Universal life has a pure insurance component (mortality protection) and a professionally managed investment component. The policyholder can pay maximum premiums and maintain a high cash value. Alternatively, the policyholder can make minimal premium payments in an amount large enough to cover mortality and other expense charges, thus not accumulating as much cash value.

Variable Life
Variable life is a form of whole life insurance with the critical difference being that the policy's cash value is invested in a segregated account comprised of equity and other securities. Premiums may be placed in the insured's choice of stock, bond, or money market funds offered through the insurance company. The death benefit and cash value of the policy depend upon the performance of the underlying investment portfolio, thus shifting the investment risk to the policyholder. There is generally, however, a minimum guaranteed death benefit. The policy allows for tax-deferred appreciation of the accumulated assets. Because variable life policies are classified as securities, life insurance agents selling these policies must also be registered representatives of a broker-dealer licensed by the National Association of Securities Dealers Regulation (NASDR) and registered with the Securities and Exchange Commission (SEC).

Variable Universal Life
Variable universal life combines the flexible premium features of universal life with the investment component of variable life. These products also are classified as securities and subject to SEC and NASD requirements.

Accident and Health Insurance

Accident and health insurance, generally referred to merely as "health insurance," is defined as insurance against loss by sickness or accidental bodily injury. The loss may be lost wages caused by the sickness or accident, or it may be expenses for doctor bills, hospital bills, medicine, and so forth. Included within this definition is insurance that provides lump sum or periodic payments, such as disability income insurance and accidental death and dismemberment in the event of loss occasioned by sickness or accident. Although these types of insurance can be written for individual coverage, most coverage is underwritten on a group basis to make premiums cost effective.

Group Life and Health Insurance
Many people are covered under group policies usually sponsored through their employers. Group plans provide low-cost insurance, and coverage is offered to everyone in the group regardless of their age or health status. Group plans have some disadvantages. There is no guarantee that the plan will be continued, and if an employee is terminated or resigns, the coverage will end. It is possible to convert group coverage to individual coverage; however, converting can be expensive for the insured.

Disability and Employment

Disability insurance is designed to replace a portion of a borrower's income, when the borrower is disabled by a covered condition. Similarly, unemployment insurance provides a portion of income, for a limited period of time, to a policyholder that subsequently becomes unemployed.

Property and Liability Insurance

Property insurance insures the policyholder against physical damage to or loss of personal or commercial property, such as homes, automobiles, and business property. Most property insurance policies require the insured to share in the loss in the form of a deductible or coinsurance.

Liability insurance protects the insured against loss resulting from being found legally liable for an injury to another person or damage to property of others. Most liability policies provide for payment of sums that the insured becomes legally obligated to pay (for the medical expenses of those injured and any damage to property of others), subject to limits. It is also typical of insuring agreements to promise defense of the insured and to reserve the right to make an out-of-court settlement. Professional liability insurance protects the insured from loss brought about by a failure to use due care and the degree of skill expected of a person in a particular situation. Malpractice insurance and errors and omissions insurance are examples of professional liability insurance.

Reinsurance

Reinsurance is a device whereby an original insurer reduces its underwriting risk by transferring all or part of the risk under an insurance policy or a group of policies to another company or insurer. Reinsurance can provide the original insurer protection against catastrophic unexpected losses. In addition, reinsurance can enable an insurance company to expand its underwriting capacity, stabilize its underwriting results, and finance its expanding volume.

The original insurer is called the direct writer, ceding company or cedant, and the recipient of the transferred risk is known as the reinsurer. The original insurer typically retains only a portion of the risk and reinsures the balance with a second underwriter. The reinsurer assumes a portion of the risk and in return receives a portion of the premium from the ceding company.

State insurance regulators generally conduct examinations every three to five years, but may examine a company when deemed necessary. The examinations focus primarily on solvency of reinsurers and their cedants and the collectibility of the reinsurance asset. A reputable reinsurer will be licensed (not all states require licensing), well capitalized, and prompt-paying.

Most insurers are licensed in one or more states to write insurance or reinsurance business. A licensed reinsurer typically must satisfy at least the same financial, reporting and examination requirements applied to primary insurers by the state insurance regulators. Some states have more stringent financial standards for reinsurers than for original insurers.

The credit for reinsurance laws, regulations, and standards typically provide that a ceding insurer cannot treat reinsurance recoverables as an asset on its financial statements unless the reinsurer meets certain tests. In general, a ceding insurer can take credit if the reinsurer is licensed or accredited in the ceding insurer's state of domicile. A large number of states and the NAIC model law on credit for reinsurance recognize well-capitalized reinsurers domiciled in another state with substantially similar laws, as well as reinsurers that maintain large trust asset accounts in the U.S. If the reinsurer does not meet those standards, the ceding insurer must treat the recoverable as a liability that can be reduced only by acceptable security—usually a letter of credit, trust fund, or amounts withheld by the ceding insurer. The requirements vary, but both the NAIC model law and the versions of the model law enacted in many states reflect a movement toward higher and more uniform standards.

Reinsurance Contracts

There are two basic methods of reinsuring or "ceding" risks to a reinsurer. The more common method is treaty reinsurance, which accounts for about 80 percent of the placements in the U.S., and the less common is facultative reinsurance. Under a treaty reinsurance contract, the reinsurer underwrites part or all of a ceding company's book of business for one or more specific classes of business. The reinsurer is generally automatically bound to reinsure any business the company writes within these specified classes. Under a facultative reinsurance contract, the ceding company cedes risk under individual policies to a reinsurer, rather than all risks within a particular class. This method reduces the ceding company's exposure to a loss on an individual risk basis, because each facultative certificate is separately negotiated.

Whether treaty or facultative, reinsurance contracts can be structured on a proportional or non-proportional (excess of loss) basis. Proportional reinsurance allows for a sharing of risk, or it may result in an increase to the primary insurer's surplus, thus allowing the primary insurer to write more business. In quota share agreements, the ceding company and the reinsurer share in the premiums and losses of each policy the company cedes on a fixed percentage basis. A facultative certificate written on a quota share basis would work similarly, but on an individual risk, rather than a whole book basis. Surplus share agreements allow the company greater flexibility in ceding risks to the reinsurer. The ceding company selects the proportion of liability it wishes to retain on any one risk or policy and may then cede multiples, known as lines, of its retention to the reinsurer. Losses and premiums are divided between the ceding company and the reinsurer in the proportion each shares in the individual risk. These agreements are generally issued only on a treaty basis.

Non-proportional or excess of loss agreements require that the primary insurer pay, and be solely responsible for, claims arising from a given book of business up to a predetermined amount, known as retention. The reinsurer is obligated to reimburse the primary insurer's claims up to another predetermined amount above retention. Thereafter, the primary insurer is solely responsible for claims in excess of the reinsurer's tier of losses on a given book. When assessing risks, examiners should consider whether the reinsurer is operating under a proportional or non-proportional agreement.

Retrocessions are reinsurance agreements that protect reinsurers for business they have assumed. These agreements, in effect, are reinsurance for reinsurers. Generally reinsurers will use retrocessional agreements to cover a larger number of reinsurance agreements to obtain the coverage needed. For example, if a reinsurer has reinsurance contracts with 12 insurance companies, only four retrocession agreements may provide needed coverage. These agreements are usually worded broadly to ensure intended coverage of all losses, and to avoid conflicts with terminology used in the various underlying reinsurance contracts.

Insurance Customer Protections

Part 14 of 12 CFR implements section 305 of GLBA. Banks must comply with the insurance consumer protection rule published under 12 CFR 14. This regulation applies to retail sales practices, solicitations, advertising, or offers of any insurance product or annuity by a depository institution or any person that is engaged in such activities at an office of the institution or on its behalf. The OCC does not consider debt cancellation contracts or debt suspension agreements as insurance; consequently, they are not governed by 12 CFR 14.

Part 14 applies to "covered persons." A covered person includes a bank; a person that sells, solicits, advertises, or offers an insurance product or annuity to a consumer at an office of the bank; or a person that sells, solicits, advertises, or offers an insurance product or annuity to a consumer on behalf of the bank. To determine compliance with this rule, a consumer is an individual who purchases, applies to purchase, or is solicited to purchase from a covered person insurance products or annuities primarily for personal, family, or household purposes. Small businesses are not consumers under this regulation. A person is acting on behalf of the bank when the person represents that the sale is on behalf of the bank; when the bank refers a customer to a seller of insurance, and the bank has a contractual relationship to receive commissions or fees derived from the sale of an insurance product or annuity resulting from that referral; or when documents evidencing the sale, solicitation, advertising, or offer of the insurance product or annuity identify or refer to the bank. An office is the premises of a bank where retail deposits are accepted from the public.

The rule prohibits misrepresentation. Banks often disseminate information to bank customers and the general public describing insurance products that are available from the bank, its subsidiaries or affiliates, or unaffiliated third parties. Banks also communicate with their customers about how to obtain more information on insurance products. To comply with 12 CFR 14, those communications must not suggest or convey any inaccurate information and should be designed with care to avoid misunderstanding, confusion, or misrepresentation to the bank's customers. Covered persons, including banks, may not engage in any practice or use any advertisement at any office of, or on behalf of, the bank or a subsidiary of the bank that could mislead any person or otherwise cause a reasonable person to reach an erroneous belief for:

- The uninsured nature of any insurance product or annuity offered for sale.

- An insurance product or annuity that involves investment risk, (the fact that there is an investment risk, including the potential that principal may be lost and that the product may decline in value).

- The fact that the approval of an extension of credit (when insurance products or annuities are sold or offered for sale) may not be conditioned on the purchase of an insurance product or annuity from the bank or its affiliates and that the consumer is free to purchase the product from another source.

The rule also requires the following affirmative disclosures, except when the disclosures would not be accurate:

- In connection with the initial purchase of an insurance product or annuity, the following disclosures must be provided orally and in writing before completion of the initial sale to the consumer.

    (1) The insurance product or annuity is not a deposit or other obligation of, or guaranteed by the bank or an affiliate of the bank.

    (2) The insurance product or annuity is not insured by the FDIC or any other agency of the United States, the bank, or an affiliate of the bank.

    (3) If there is an insurance product or annuity that involves an investment risk, there is investment risk associated with the product, including the possible loss of value.

- In connection with an application for credit in which an insurance product or annuity is solicited, offered, or sold, banks must disclose that the bank may not condition an extension of credit on either:

    (1) The consumer's purchase of an insurance product or annuity from the bank or any of its affiliates; or

(2) The consumer's agreement not to obtain, or a prohibition on the consumer from obtaining, an insurance product or annuity from an unaffiliated entity.

In most cases, these disclosures must be made orally and in writing at the time the consumer applies for an extension of credit that is associated with an insurance product or annuity that is solicited, offered, or sold. There are various exceptions to this requirement for mail, telephone, and electronic transactions.

(1) Mail — Oral disclosures are not required if the sale of the insurance product or the application for credit is taken by mail.

(2) Telephone — If the sale is conducted by telephone, a covered person may provide the written insurance disclosures by mail within three business days beginning on the first business day after the sale. A covered person may also provide the written credit disclosure by mail if the covered person mails it to the consumer within three days beginning the first business day after the credit application is taken.

(3) Electronic disclosures — A covered person may provide the written insurance and credit disclosures through electronic media if the customer affirmatively consents to receiving the disclosures electronically, and the consumer can download the disclosures in a form that can be retained later, such as by printing or storing electronically.

All disclosures must be readily understandable and meaningful. Disclosures must be conspicuous, simple, direct, readily understandable, and designed to call attention to the nature and significance of the information provided. Examples of meaningful disclosures include plain language headings, easy-to-read typeface and type-size, wide margins, boldface or italics for key words, and distinctive type styles. Disclosures are not meaningfully provided in the electronic context if the consumer can bypass the visual text of the disclosures before purchasing the product.

Certain short form disclosures may be used in visual media and, as appropriate, in other circumstances. For example, a covered person may use the following disclosures in visual media:

- NOT A DEPOSIT
- NOT FDIC-INSURED
- NOT INSURED BY ANY FEDERAL GOVERNMENT AGENCY
- NOT GUARANTEED BY THE BANK
- MAY GO DOWN IN VALUE

Banks must also obtain written acknowledgement from the consumer that he/she received the required disclosures. The acknowledgement must be received at the time the consumer receives the disclosures or before the initial sale.

Banks must, to the extent practicable, keep the area where it conducts its insurance and annuities transactions physically segregated from areas where retail deposits are routinely accepted from the general public. In addition to physical segregation, the rule also requires the bank to identify the areas where the sales activity occurs and to distinguish those areas from the areas where the bank's retail deposit taking activities occur. (The area where retail deposits are routinely accepted generally means traditional teller windows and teller lines.)

Any person accepting deposits from the public, in an area where such transactions are routinely conducted in the bank, may refer a consumer who seeks to purchase an insurance product or annuity to a qualified person who sells that product. If the bank has a referral fee program, the referral fee paid to this person may not be more than a one-time, nominal fee of a fixed dollar amount that does not depend on whether the referral results in a transaction.

These examination procedures can be used when performing the additional risk assessment. These procedures are used, when in the examiner's judgment, they are necessary to determine the level of compliance with 12 CFR 14, to determine the quality of the bank's compliance program, or because the OCC has identified or suspects violations.

Objective: Determine the bank's level of compliance with 12 CFR 14, Consumer Protection in Sales of Insurance.

1. Select samples of initial sales of insurance and annuities and credit applications when insurance or an annuity is solicited by the applicant, or offered or sold to the applicant by the bank or covered person (include sales made and loan applications received by telephone, mail, and electronic media). Also select a sample of advertisements and promotional materials for the sale of insurance and annuities.

2. Review the samples, consumer complaint information, and audit findings and determine whether:

    a. Before completion of the initial sale, consumers received and acknowledged receipt of information disclosing the fact that the insurance or annuity [12 CFR 14.40(c)(1) and (c)(7)]:

        • Is not a deposit or other obligation of, or guaranteed by, the bank or an affiliate of the bank [12 CFR 14.40(a)(1)].

        • Is not insured by the Federal Deposit Insurance Corporation or any other agency of the United States, the bank or a bank affiliate [12 CFR 14.40(a)(2)].

        • May involve investment risk, including the possible loss of value, if applicable [12 CFR 14.40(a)(3)].

    b. At the time the consumer applied for credit, the consumer received and acknowledged (at that time or at the time of the sale) receipt of information disclosing the fact that the bank may not condition a credit extension on [12 CFR 14.40(c)(1) and (c)(7)]:

- Purchase of an insurance product or annuity from the bank or any of its affiliates [12 CFR 14.40(b)(1)].

- Agreement not to obtain, or a prohibition on the consumer from obtaining, an insurance product or annuity from an unaffiliated entity [12 CFR 14.40(b)(2)].

    c.   Advertisements and promotional materials include the disclosures described in 2a, [12 CFR 14.40(d)].

    d.   The bank led the consumer to believe that in obtaining a loan from the bank, the consumer must purchase insurance or an annuity from the bank or its affiliates, or the consumer must agree not to purchase insurance or an annuity from a non-affiliate [12 CFR 14.30(a)].

    e.   The bank led the consumer to believe that the insurance product was backed by the federal government or bank, was insured by the FDIC, or when an investment risk existed, that the product did not involve an investment risk [12 CFR 14.30(b)].

    f.   The bank considered the status of the consumer as victim of domestic violence, or provider of services to victims of domestic violence, as a criterion in any decision for insurance underwriting, pricing, renewal, scope of coverage, or payment of claims [12 CFR 14.30(c)].

3.   Review the disclosures in 2a and 2b, and determine whether they were conspicuous, simple, direct, readily understandable, designed to call attention to the nature and significance of the information provided, and provided in a meaningful form [12 CFR 14.40(c)(5) and (c)(6)].

4.   Through discussions with insurance sales personnel and a review of the bank's training program, determine whether sales personnel provide, and are trained to provide, disclosures orally and in writing prior to completion of the initial sale and at the time a consumer applies for credit (in connection with insurance solicitations, offerings, or sales) [12 CFR 14.40(c)(1)].

5.   Through discussions with management and on-site inspection, determine whether the bank physically segregates and identifies such areas within the bank where it conducts insurance product and annuity transactions and where it conducts retail deposit-taking activities [12 CFR 14.50(a)].

6.   Review the bank's compensation program for insurance referrals and select a sample of employee compensation records (employees who accept deposits from the public in an area where such transactions are routinely conducted in the bank and make referrals to others for the sale of insurance products or annuities). Verify that such employees receive no more than a one-time, nominal fee of a fixed dollar amount for each referral, and that payment of this fee does not depend on whether the referral results in a transaction [12 CFR 14.50(b)].

7.   Select a sample of persons who sell or offer for sale any insurance product or annuity in any part of the bank or on its behalf. Determine whether each person has always been qualified and licensed appropriately under applicable state insurance licensing standards for the specific products they sell or recommend [12 CFR 14.60].

Conclusions

Objective: Prepare written conclusion summaries, discuss findings with the EIC, and communicate findings to management. If necessary, identify needed corrective action when policies or internal controls are deficient or when violations of law or regulation are identified.

1. Summarize findings and violations from the preceding procedural steps to assess the bank's level of compliance with 12 CFR 14, Consumer Protection in Sales of Insurance.

2. For those violations found to be significant or a pattern or practice, determine their root cause by identifying weaknesses in:

   - Internal controls.
   - Audit/independent compliance review.
   - Training.
   - Management oversight.

3. Determine whether civil money penalties (CMP) or an enforcement action should be recommended (refer to the CMP matrix).

4. Identify action needed to correct violations and weaknesses in the institution's compliance system.

5. Determine whether any items identified during this examination could evolve into supervisory concerns before the next on-site examination, considering whether the bank has plans to increase monitoring in the affected area, or anticipates changes in personnel, policy, outside auditors or consultants, or business strategy. If so, summarize your concerns and assess the potential risk to the bank.

6. Determine the effect on aggregate risk and direction of risk for any concerns identified during the review. Examiners should refer to guidance provided under the OCC's large and community bank risk assessment programs.

   - Risk categories: compliance, transaction, reputation.
   - Risk conclusions: high, moderate, or low.
   - Risk direction: increasing, stable, or declining.

7. Form a conclusion about the reliability of the compliance management system for Consumer Protection in Sales of Insurance and provide conclusions to the examiner performing the Compliance Management System program.

8. Provide, and discuss with, the EIC (and the supervisory office, if appropriate) conclusions, including:

   - A summary of violations and recommended CMPs or enforcement actions, if any.
   - Recommended corrective action.
   - The quantity of risk and quality of risk management.
   - Recommended MRAs.

     – MRAs should cover practices that:
       - Deviate from sound fundamental principles and are likely to result in financial deterioration, if not addressed.
       - Result in substantive noncompliance with laws.

     – MRAs should discuss:
       - Causative factors contributing to the problem.
       - Consequences of inaction.
       - Management's commitment for corrective action.
       - The time frame and person(s) responsible for corrective action.

9. Discuss findings with management. Obtain commitment(s) for corrective action as needed. Include in the discussion:

   - The quantity of risk and quality or risk management.
   - Violations of 12 CFR 14.
   - MRAs.

10. As appropriate, prepare a brief comment for inclusion in the report of examination.

11. Prepare a memorandum summarizing work performed (sampling method used, internal control systems, scope of audit review, conclusions regarding audit, etc.) and update the work program with any information that will facilitate future examinations. Update the OCC database on all violations of law or regulation.

12.   Organize and reference working papers in accordance with OCC guidance (PPM 5400-8).

Privacy Rule — 12 CFR 40 and the Fair Credit Reporting Act

Banks must provide their customers an annual privacy notice in addition to the initial privacy notices discussed in the main body of this booklet. All privacy notices must be clear and conspicuous, and must be provided so that each intended recipient can reasonably be expected to receive actual notice. The notices must be in writing (unless the consumer agrees to electronic delivery) and must describe the types of nonpublic personal information collected and disclosed, the types of affiliated and nonaffiliated third parties with whom the information may be shared, and, if applicable, the consumer's right to opt out and thereby limit certain information sharing by the bank.

Banks generally may not, directly or through an affiliate, disclose a consumer's nonpublic personal information to any nonaffiliated third party unless the consumer is given a reasonable opportunity to direct that such information not be disclosed, i.e., to opt out. Before a bank may disclose nonpublic personal information about a consumer to a nonaffiliated third party, the bank must provide the consumer with an initial privacy notice and an opt-out notice. GLBA contains a number of specific exceptions to these opt-out requirements, however, to ensure that banks can continue to disclose information to nonaffiliated third parties to conduct routine business. These exceptions include, for instance, the disclosure of information by banks to third parties who are providing services to the bank or to their customers as the bank's agent.

The interagency rule also provides that a bank generally may not disclose a credit card, deposit, or transaction account number of a consumer to any nonaffiliated third party for use in telemarketing, direct mail, or other marketing through electronic mail to the consumer. The rule also limits the redisclosure or reuse of information obtained from other nonaffiliated financial institutions.

Functionally regulated subsidiaries that sell insurance must comply with state laws and regulations that govern the handling of consumer information, such as health information, in connection with insurance activities. Under GLBA, state insurance authorities are expected to promulgate privacy regulations that apply to insurance companies. States could, for example, adopt the NAIC's model privacy regulation that requires all licensees of a state insurance department to obtain specific consumer authorization (opt in) before disclosing health information.

The disclosure of certain consumer information may also trigger requirements under the Fair Credit Reporting Act (FCRA). Although the FCRA imposes no limits on a bank's disclosure to third parties of information about the bank's transactions and experiences with its customers, the FCRA governs the sharing of credit reports and other information that meets the statutory definition of "consumer report." The FCRA provides that banks and other entities may share such information among their affiliates without being considered consumer reporting agencies if they provide their consumers with notice about the sharing and an opportunity to opt out. Banks engaged in insurance sales activities should consider the applicability of the FCRA and any regulations that may be promulgated before disclosing "consumer report" information.

For additional information on the provisions of part 40 and the FCRA and how they relate, see OCC Bulletin 2000-25, "Privacy Laws and Regulations," September 8, 2000 (available on the OCC's Web site at http://www.occ.treas.gov/OCC_current.htm).

Federal Prohibitions on Tying

Under 12 USC 1972, federal law prohibits certain tying arrangements. The statute's implementing regulation (12 CFR 225.7) provides some exceptions to the statutory tying restrictions for banks, including national banks. The exceptions permit certain tying arrangements for national banks and are applicable to national bank operating subsidiaries. For purposes of the federal tying prohibitions, a national bank financial subsidiary is considered a subsidiary of the bank holding company and not the bank, as provided in 12 USC 1971 (also see 12 CFR 5.39(h)(6)). Thus, the general tying restrictions applicable to national banks and their operating subsidiaries are not applicable to financial subsidiaries. A financial subsidiary is subject to the limited tying prohibition in 12 CFR 225.7(d) involving tying electronic benefit transfer services to other point-of-sale services. Tying arrangements may violate other laws, including the federal antitrust laws, in addition to anti-tying provisions.

OCC Bulletin 95-20, "Tying Restrictions," describes measures banks can take that help to ensure compliance with the tying prohibitions. The measures include:

- Monitoring to eliminate impermissible coercion when offering customers multiple products or services.

- Training bank employees about the tying prohibitions, including providing examples of prohibited practices and sensitizing employees to the concerns raised by tying.

- Involving management in reviewing training, audit, and compliance programs, and updating any policies and procedures to reflect changes in products, services, or applicable law.

- Reviewing customer files to determine whether any extension of credit is conditioned impermissibly on obtaining an insurance product from the bank or affiliates.

- Monitoring incentives, such as commissions and fee splitting arrangements, that may encourage tying.

- Responding to any customer allegations of prohibited tying arrangements.

In situations involving sales of insurance in connection with extending a loan, banks must also comply with the requirements of 12 CFR 14. In summary, Part 14 prohibits engagement in any practice that would lead a consumer to believe that an extension of credit is conditional upon:

- The purchase of an insurance product or annuity from the bank or any of its affiliates.

- An agreement by the consumer not to obtain, or a prohibition on the consumer from obtaining, an insurance product or annuity from an unaffiliated entity.

Tying prohibitions do not prevent bank sales personnel from informing a customer that insurance is required to obtain a loan or that loan approval is contingent on the customer obtaining acceptable insurance. In such circumstances, sales personnel may indicate that insurance is available from the bank and may provide instructions on how the customer can obtain additional information. However, the bank should clarify to the customer that the bank's decisions on a loan application are independent of the customer's decision on where to obtain insurance.

Tying concerns are equally pertinent and potentially more acute if a type of insurance that is unrelated to, or not required in connection with, a pending loan application is offered to a loan applicant as part of the loan application process. In that situation, banks should use great care to dispel any impression that the unrelated products are being mentioned because of a potential connection to the bank's credit decision. The bank should ensure that, if such offers are permitted, they are monitored adequately by the bank's compliance system.

This glossary is not a complete listing of all terminology related to insurance products or services. It does provide descriptions of insurance products that banks are most likely to offer and definitions of terms associated with them.

Accident and Health Insurance: A type of coverage that pays benefits in case of sickness, accidental injury, or accidental death. This coverage may provide for loss of income or debt payment if taken out in conjunction with a loan.

Actuary: A person professionally trained in the technical aspects of insurance and related fields, such as pension plans or annuity products. An actuary uses mathematics to calculate premiums, reserves, and other insurance-related values.

Agent: A licensed insurance company representative under contract to one or more insurance companies. Agents generally are compensated by commissions on policies sold, although some may receive salaries. Depending on the line of insurance represented, an agent's power may include creating and effecting coverage, such as with property insurance, or primarily selling and servicing contracts, as with life insurance. Agents are most commonly described in terms of the contractual relationship between the agent and an insurance company. An exclusive or captive agent represents only one insurer, but still may operate through the agency system. An exclusive agent is often, but not always, an employee of that insurer. A general agent is usually contractually awarded a specific geographic territory for an individual insurance company. General agents are responsible for building their own agency and usually represent only one insurer. Unlike exclusive agents, who usually receive a salary in addition to commissions, general agents are compensated on a commission basis only. An independent agent can work alone or in partnership or corporate affiliations. Under a contractual agreement, independent agents represent many different insurers in the life, health, annuity, and property and liability fields. All of their compensation originates from commissions.

Aggregate Excess Loss Reinsurance: A form of "excess of loss" reinsurance that indemnifies the ceding company against the amount by which all of the ceding company's losses incurred during a specific period (usually 12 months) exceed either (1) a predetermined dollar amount; or (2) a percentage of the company's subject premiums (loss ratio) for the specific period. This type of contract is also commonly referred to as "stop loss" reinsurance or Aexcess of loss" ratio reinsurance.

Assignment: The legal transfer of one person's interest in an insurance policy to another person or business.

Beneficiary: The person or entity named in the policy as the recipient of insurance proceeds upon the policyholder's death.

Binder: A written or oral agreement, typically issued for property and casualty insurance, to provide interim coverage pending receipt, and final acceptance, of a person's application for insurance.

Broker: A broker is an person who represents the insurance buyer, not an insurance company or agent, and assists the buyer in obtaining insurance coverage desired. Brokers do not have the power to bind an insurance company to an insurance contract. However, once a contract is accepted, the broker is compensated for the transaction through a commission from the insurance company.

Bulk Reinsurance: A transaction sometimes defined by statute as any quota share, surplus aid, or portfolio reinsurance agreement through which, of itself or in combination with other similar agreements, an insurer assumes all or a substantial portion of the liability of the reinsured company.

Captive Insurer: An insurance company established by a parent firm to insure the parent's risk exposures.

Cash Surrender Value: The amount of cash available to a policyholder upon the voluntary termination of a life insurance policy before it becomes payable by death or maturity.

Cede: To transfer to a reinsurer all or part of the insurance or reinsurance risk written by a ceding company.

Ceding Commission: In calculating a reinsurance premium, an amount allowed by the reinsurer for part or all of a ceding company's acquisition and other overhead costs, including premium taxes. It may also include a profit factor.

Ceding Company (also Cedant, Reinsured, Reassured): The insurer that cedes all or part of the insurance or reinsurance risk it has written to another insurer/reinsurer.

Cession: The amount of insurance risk transferred to the reinsurer by the ceding company.

Claim: A request for payment of a loss under the terms of a policy. Claims are payable in the manner suited to the insured risk. Life, property, casualty, health, and liability claims generally are paid in a lump sum after the loss is incurred. Disability and loss-of-time claims are paid periodically during the period of disability, or through a discounted lump sum payment.

Coinsurance: A provision found in property and casualty that requires the insured to maintain a specified amount of insurance based on the value of the property insured. Coinsurance clauses are also found in health insurance and require the insured to share a percentage of the loss.

Combination Plan Reinsurance: A reinsurance agreement that combines the excess of loss and the quota share forms of coverage within one contract, with the reinsurance premium established as a fixed percentage of the ceding company's subject premium. After deducting the excess recovery on any one loss for one risk, the reinsurer indemnifies the ceding company based on a fixed quota share percentage. If a loss does not exceed the excess of loss retention level, only the quota share coverage applies.

Comprehensive Personal Liability Insurance: A type of insurance that reimburses the policyholder if he or she becomes liable to pay money for damage or injury he or she has caused to others. This coverage does not include automobile liability but does include almost every activity of the policyholder, except business operations.

Credit for Reinsurance: A statutory accounting procedure permitting a ceding company to treat amounts due from reinsurers as assets or reductions from liabilities based on the status of the reinsurer.

Credit Life Insurance: A decreasing term insurance product issued on the life of a debtor that is tied to repayment of a specific loan or indebtedness. Proceeds of a credit life insurance policy are used to extinguish remaining indebtedness at the time of the borrower's death. The term is applied broadly to other forms of credit-related insurance that provides for debt satisfaction in the event of a borrower's disability, accident or health, and unemployment.

Deductible: The amount a policyholder agrees to pay toward the total amount of insurance loss. The deductible may apply to each claim for a loss occurrence, such as each automobile accident, or to all claims made during a specified period, as with health insurance.

Designations: Two of the most common designations are CLU (Chartered Life Underwriter) and ChFC (Chartered Financial Consultant). Insurance agents also join professional organizations such as the American Society of Chartered Life Underwriters, the International Association of Financial Planning, the National Association of Life Underwriters, the National Association of Health Underwriters, the American Council of Life Insurance, the Life Insurance Marketing and Research Association, the Life Underwriter Training Council, and the Million Dollar Round Table.

Direct Premiums Written: Premiums received for all policies written during a given time period by the insurer, excluding those received through reinsurance assumed.

Direct Writer: An insurance company that deals directly with the insured through a salaried representative, as opposed to those insurers that use agents. This term also is used to refer to insurers that operate through exclusive agents. In reinsurance, a direct writer is the company that originally underwrites insurance policies ceded.

Disability Income Insurance: An insurance product that provides income payment to the insured when income is interrupted or terminated because of illness or accident.

Errors and Omissions Liability Insurance: Professional liability insurance for people in various professions that require protection for negligent acts or omissions resulting in bodily injury, personal injury, or property damage liability to a client.

Excess of Loss Reinsurance: A form of reinsurance whereby an insurer pays the amount of each claim for each risk up to a limit determined in advance, and the reinsurer pays the amount of the claim above that limit up to a specific sum. It includes various types of reinsurance, such as catastrophe reinsurance, per risk reinsurance, per occurrence reinsurance and aggregate excess of loss reinsurance.

Excess Per Risk Reinsurance: A form of excess of loss reinsurance, which subject to a specified limit, indemnifies the ceding company against the amount of loss in excess of a specified retention for each risk involved in each occurrence.

Exposure: Aggregate of all policyholder limits of liability arising from policies written. This term also is used to define the nature of the risk insured.

Face Amount: The amount stated on the face of the insurance policy that will be paid, depending upon the type of coverage, upon death or maturity. It does not include dividend additions or additional amounts payable under accidental death or other special provisions.

Facultative Reinsurance: Reinsurance of individual risks by offer and acceptance wherein the reinsurer retains the faculty to accept or reject each risk offered by the ceding company.

Facultative Treaty: A reinsurance contract under which the ceding company has the option to cede and the reinsurer has the option to accept or decline classified risks of a specific business line. The contract merely reflects how individual facultative reinsurance shall be handled.

Financial Strength Rating: Opinion as to an insurance company's ability to meet its senior policyholder obligations and claims. For many years, the principal rating agency for both property and liability insurers and life insurers has been A.M. Best. Other rating agencies, such as Duff and Phelps, Moody's, Standard and Poor's, and Weiss, also rate insurers.

Flood Insurance: A special insurance policy to protect against the risk of loss or damage to property caused by flooding. Regular homeowners' policies do not pay for damages caused by flooding.

Gross Premiums Written: Total premiums for insurance written during a given period, before deduction for reinsurance ceded.

Group Insurance: Insurance coverage typically issued to an employer under a master policy for the benefit of employees. The insurer usually does not condition coverage of people that make up the group upon satisfactory medical examinations or other requirements. The individual members of the group hold certificates as evidence of their insurance.

Health Insurance: An insurance product that provides benefits for medical expenses incurred as a result of sickness or accident, as well as income payments to replace lost income when the insured is unable to work because of illness, accident, or disability. This product may be in the form of traditional indemnity insurance or managed care plans and may be underwritten on an individual or group basis.

Incurred But Not Reported (IBNR): The loss reserve value established by insurance and reinsurance companies in recognition of their liability for future payments on losses that have occurred, but have not yet been reported to them. This definition is often erroneously expanded to include adverse loss development on reported claims. The term, Incurred But Not Enough Reported (IBNER), is coming into increased usage to reflect more accurately the adverse development on inadequately reserved reported claims.

Key Person Life Insurance: Life insurance designed to cover the key employees of an employer. It may be written on a group or an individual policy basis.

Lapse: The termination or discontinuance of a policy, resulting from the insured's failure to pay the premium due.

Long-Term Care Insurance: Health insurance coverage designed to cover the cost of custodial care in nursing homes or extended care facilities.

Managing General Agent: A managing general agent (MGA) is a wholesaler of insurance products and services to insurance agents. An MGA receives contractual authority from an insurer to assume many of the insurance company's functions. The MGA may provide products (needed insurance coverages) to the public through local insurance agents as well as diversified services, including marketing, accounting, data processing, policy maintenance and service, and monitoring of claims. Many insurance companies prefer the MGA distribution and management system for the marketing and underwriting of their insurance products, because it avoids the high cost of establishing branch offices. Most states require that an MGA be licensed.

Multi-Peril Insurance: Insurance contract providing coverage against many perils, usually combining liability and physical damage coverage.

Net Premiums Written: The amount of gross premiums written, after deduction for premiums ceded to reinsurers.

Ninety-Day Rule: The annual statement requirement that provides that an insurer must establish a provision for certain balances when it has reinsurance recoverables over 90 days past due.

Obligatory Treaty: A reinsurance contract under which business must be ceded in accordance with contract terms and must be accepted by the reinsurer.

Policyholder: The person or entity who owns an insurance policy. This is usually the insured person, but it may also be a relative of the insured, a partnership, or a corporation.

Premium: The payment, or one of the periodic payments, a policyholder agrees to make for insurance coverage.

Private Mortgage Insurance: Private mortgage insurance, or PMI, protects the mortgage lender against losses due to a collateral shortfall on a defaulted residential real estate loan. Most banks require borrowers to take out a PMI policy if a down payment of less than 20 percent of a home's value is made at the time the loan is originated. PMI does not directly benefit a borrower, although its existence provides the opportunity to purchase a home to many people who otherwise would not qualify for a loan.

Pro Rata Reinsurance: A generic term describing all forms of "quota share" and "surplus reinsurance," in which the reinsurer shares a pro rata portion of the losses and premiums of the ceding company.

Property Damage: Physical injury to, or destruction of, tangible property that occurs during the policy period. Examples are fire, windstorm, motor vehicles, explosion, and vandalism.

Quota Share Reinsurance: A form of pro rata reinsurance, indemnifying the ceding company for a fixed percent of loss on each risk covered in the contract in consideration of the same percentage of the premium paid to the ceding company.

Rebating: Directly or indirectly giving or offering to give any portion of the premium or any other consideration to an insurance buyer as an inducement to purchase or renew the insurance. Rebates are forbidden under most state insurance codes.

Reinsurance: Insurance placed by an underwriter in another company to cut down the amount of the risk assumed under the original insurance.

Reinsurance Premium: The consideration paid by a ceding company to a reinsurer for the coverage provided by the reinsurer.

Retrocession: A reinsurance transaction whereby a reinsurer (the retrocedant) cedes all or part of the reinsurance risks it has assumed to another reinsurer (the retrocessionaire).

Rider: A written attachment, also known as an endorsement, to an insurance policy that changes the original policy to meet specific requirements, such as increasing/decreasing benefits or providing coverage for specific property items beyond that provided for under the insurance company=s standard contract terms.

Term Life Insurance: Insurance product that provides, for a specified period of time, death coverage only. Typically, it has no savings component and, therefore, no cash value. Because term insurance provides only mortality protection, it generally provides the most coverage per premium dollar. Most term life insurance policies are renewable for one or more time periods; however, premiums generally increase with the age of the policyholder.

Title Insurance: Insurance that protects banks and mortgagees against unknown encumbrances against real estate by indemnifying the mortgagor and property owner in the event that clear ownership of the property is clouded by the discovery of faults in the title. Title insurance policies may be issued to either the mortgagor or the mortgagee or both. Title insurance is written largely only by companies specializing in this class of insurance.

Treaty: A reinsurance contract under which the reinsured company agrees to cede, and the reinsurer agrees to assume, risks of a particular class or classes of business.

Twisting: Twisting involves inducing a policyholder to terminate a policy with one company and to take out a policy with another company, when it is not to the insured's benefit to do so. Twisting is similar to the "churning" concept in securities sales, and it results in increased commissions for the inducing agent.

Unearned Reinsurance Premium: That part of the reinsurance premium applicable to the unexpired portion of the policies reinsured.

Underwriting: The process by which a company determines whether it can accept an application for insurance, and, if so, on what basis. For example, the underwriting process for life insurance classifies applicants by identifying such characteristics as age, sex, health, occupation, and hobbies. People with similar characteristics are grouped together and are charged a premium based on the group's level of risk. The process rejects unacceptable risks.

Universal Life Insurance: A form of permanent insurance designed to provide flexibility in premium payments and death benefit protection. The policyholder can pay maximum premiums and maintain a high cash value. Alternatively, the policyholder can make minimal payments in an amount only large enough to cover mortality and other expense charges.

Variable Life Insurance: A form of whole life or universal life when the policyholder's cash value is supported by assets segregated from the general asset structure of the insurance company. The policyholder assumes all investment and price risk. Because variable life policies have investment features, life insurance agents selling these policies must be registered representatives of a broker-dealer licensed by the National Association of Securities Dealers and registered with the Securities and Exchange Commission.

Vendors Single Interest Insurance: A form of force-placed insurance that is typically purchased by the bank to protect against loss or damage to loan collateral in which the bank has a security interest. The bank passes its expense for this insurance on to the consumer who has either refused or is unable to obtain property insurance.

Whole Life Insurance: A fixed rate insurance product, with premiums and death benefits guaranteed over the duration of the policy. There is a cash value (essentially a savings account) that accrues to the policyholder tax-deferred. A policyholder receives the cash value in lieu of death benefits if the policy matures or lapses before the insured's death. A policyholder also may borrow against the policy's accumulated cash value or use it to pay future premiums. Premiums are constant for the life of the insured contract for most whole life insurance policies.

Laws

Gramm-Leach-Bliley Act, Section 104 and Title III — Insurance
12 USC 24 (Seventh), Corporate Powers of Associations
12 USC 24a, Financial Subsidiaries
12 USC 92, Acting as Insurance Agent or Broker
12 USC 371c, Banking Affiliates
12 USC 371c-1, Restrictions on Transactions with Affiliates
12 USC 1861 through 1867, Bank Service Corporation Act
12 USC 1972, Certain Tying Arrangements Prohibited; Correspondent Accounts
12 USC 2601-17, Real Estate Settlement Procedures Act of 1974
15 USC 1681-1681t, Fair Credit Reporting Act

Regulations

12 CFR 2, Sales of Credit Life Insurance
12 CFR 5, Financial Subsidiaries and Operating Subsidiaries
12 CFR 7.1001, National Bank Acting As General Insurance Agent
12 CFR 1, 14, Consumer Protection in Sales of Insurance
12 CFR 40, Privacy of Consumer Financial Information
12 CFR 225.7, Exceptions to Tying Restrictions
12 CFR 226, Truth in Lending
24 CFR 3500, Real Estate Settlement Procedures Act

OCC Issuances

OCC Bulletin 95-20, "Tying Restrictions"
OCC Bulletin 2000-16, "Risk Modeling"
OCC Bulletin 2000-25, "Privacy Laws and Regulations"
OCC Bulletin 2001-43, "Consumer Protections for Depository Institution Sales of Insurance" (Interagency Guidance on 12 CFR 14)
OCC Bulletin 2001-47, "Risk Management Principles for Third-Party Relationships"

Other Reference Sources

OTS Handbook
FRB Handbook
NAIC Examiner Handbook
Vaughan, Emmett J. and Therese M. Vaughan, Fundamentals of Risk
and Insurance, John Wiley and Sons, Inc., 1996.
NAC Corporation. Reinsurance Contracts — Content and Regulation.
NAC Corporation, 1996.
FEMA, Mandatory Purchase of Flood Insurance Guidelines.